LIAM SWORDS

Topical
Homilies

the columba press

the columba press

Lower Kilmacud Road, Blackrock, Co. Dublin, Ireland

First Edition 1987
Designed by Bill Bolger
Typeset Koinonia Ltd, Manchester
Printed in Ireland by
Mount Salus Press, Dublin

ISBN 0-948183-43-8

Contents

iii

v

The End

Liturgical Year Index

Index of Themes

Introduction

If you can keep your head . . .

They're saying it at last! And those who are not saying it are thinking it. 'Religion is going in this country.' Parents are saying it – they see it in their children. Teachers are saying it – the classroom is full of protest and barricades. Old people are saying it – understandably. It is probably nostalgia. The young people are saying it – possibly triumphantly. The headlines have it – Drugs in City! Aids an epidemic? Drop in church attendance among the young. Maoists in the town! They can't all be wrong. There is no smoke without a fire.

Undoubtedly things are changing. In what direction is open to argument. But change itself is a new and dominating factor in our lives. The inability of many to cope with change is their greatest problem. Religion is more resistant to change than any other aspect of life. Many regard it as the only anchor left in a rapidly changing world. To them its changelessness is its most attractive quality. Nothing frightens them more than the suggestion of a changing religion.

And so they react, sometimes violently, to any attempts at adapting religion to meet modern needs. Their reactions vary. Some refuse to believe the evidence of their own eyes. Nothing is new. What changes there are, are few and superficial. They are best ignored. If you pretend you don't see them, they might go away. Student unrest and urban guerillas are the creation of news-hungry mass-media. What youthful rebellion does exist is dismissed with the observation 'Young people were always rebellious'.

And then there are those who believe they know the explanation of all the unrest. And a problem explained is a problem solved. Whether it be increased industrial strikes, or the job crisis, or liberation theology their explanation is all-embracing. It is an international Communist plot. For those of us reared in the time of the Stalinist purges, on a diet of Cold War propaganda, in an atmosphere thick with the intrigues of international espionage, it is not easy to dismiss such an explanation.

Those who harp back with nostalgia to the good old days when 'sex was dirty and the air was clean' have their answer for all our

1

problems. It has all the charm of simplicity. Bring back the big stick. What the world needs now is not love, sweet love but good old fashioned authority (or tyranny as it was known then). More parental authority in the home, no-nonsense teachers in the class-room, more police in the streets. If it worked in the past, it will work now.

There is no turning the clock back. Change is the climate we live in and the greatest problem we have to cope with. There is no one single explanation of it, as indeed there is no one simple solution. And there is no evidence to support the idea that given time, as many hope, all will settle down again. The opposite is at least as probable – an accelerating rate of change in the future.

Do you feel threatened by guitars in church or nuns in lay attire or the prospect of a married clergy? If you do, you need to strengthen your faith in the essentials. You must throw away the pretty box your religion came in. You have probably held on to it too tightly for too long.

Kipling summed it up in verse:

If you can keep you head when all about you
Are losing theirs, and blaming it on you. . .
Yours is the earth and everything that's in it,
And – which is more – you'll be a Man, my son.

Cardinal Newman gave it a religious slant:

In a higher world it is otherwise,
But here below to live is to change,
And to be perfect is to have changed often.

Home

Open to life

Life offers no more awesome change than the transition from singlehood to parenthood. None of life's other experiences is so marvellously profound, so totally transforming. From girlhood to motherhood, from boyhood to fatherhood is an implosion into a new orbit. Parents become pro-Creators. God the Father graciously elicits their cooperation in a new creation. Their love is no longer turned inward on themselves but outward and open to life. And God said: 'Let us make man in our own image and likeness'. The fruit of their love is the image of all three, of father, of mother and God.

'Therefore, a man leaves his father and mother and cleaves to his wife and they become one flesh.' They mortgage themselves and their lives on a new home. Home is the warm love that breeds new life, cradles it through its vulnerable years and nurtures it for the outside world's harsher climate. Together, father and mother build a home, warm and comforting, strong and secure.

By wisdom a house is built,
and by understanding it is established;
by knowledge the rooms are filled
with all precious and pleasant riches (Prov 4:3-4)

The 'precious riches' make demands, demands only love could bear. Painful moments, fretful hours, anxious days, sleepless nights. Knowledge is being there to hold a sick child's hand. Understanding is wiping away the tears and being rewarded with a smile. Wisdom is double-edged. Children learn to grow up and parents rediscover their childhood. Home is the centre of this world and the promise of a better world to come.

Homelessness defines the needy, the lonely, the abandoned and the marginalised. Only home can fill their need. The nuclear family blossoms into the extended family, to share its warmth with the less fortunate. The word *home* is an acronym with a moral. H stands for happiness. O stands for others. ME signifies self. The secret of a happy home is always to put others before self. Husband puts his wife first, and she her husband. Both put their children first and they their parents. All put neighbours first, especially those most in need. Small wonder Christ chose the virtues of home for entry into the heavenly home:

'I was hungry and you gave me food, I was thirsty and you gave me drink, I was a stranger and you welcomed me, I was naked and you clothed me, I was sick and you visited me, I was in prison and you came to me' (Mt 25: 35-36).

Children always assume their parents go to heaven. They should know with their privileged information. To parents, their children were 'the least of the brethren'.

That family feeling

I was always under the impression that the quality of family life in Ireland was second to none. I've had second thoughts since I started travelling abroad. I've had a chance of observing at fairly close range families in London, New York, San Francisco and France and I've been quite surprised to find how tightly knit they are. In these countries the evening meal is the big meal and all the family from those in their late teens or early twenties down to the toddlers take part. It's a family occasion. Evening is family time. Rarely is any member missing. Very occasionally and then only for very important reasons is any member excused. And after dinner the whole family enjoy the evening together. 'Going out' is very much the exception. I was intrigued watching father spending his evening playing chess with his 18 year-old son. And they were both obviously enjoying themselves. Nobody seemed to want a life of his own. They were quite happy to be part of a family.

Not family-Irish-style, I think you'll agree. Children have scarcely reached their teens here, when they begin to go their own way. There is almost an indecent haste about the way 14 and 15 year-olds shed their families. They find their own pals in school and clubs and make their own entertainment roaming the streets. Home is only where they sleep and get their meals. I remember when I was a teenager getting a seat to football matches on Sundays with a pal in his father's car. As soon as we got there our first job was to lose the 'oul fella'. Not very hard done indeed. He was just as keen to lose us after the match while he slipped away for a few quick ones. Whatever about mothers and daughters, fathers and sons, especially older sons, don't share much of their leisure together and when they do it's always out of a sense of duty. I think most teenage boys find their families a bit of an embarrassment really. The less they interfere with his life the happier he is. And it's all regarded as very normal. In fact the boy who spends a lot of time with his family and enjoys it, is regarded as a bit of a cissy.

Of course, it's easy to see why families abroad are much closer-knit than here. They exist in a vicious fear-ridden society. The ten o'clock news in New York begins every night with the words, 'Do you know where your children are?' A constant reminder that it's not safe for any of them to be outside their homes at that hour. The nightly toil of murders, rapes and robberies with violence in New York would make Belfast look a very quiet place. Incidentally, the 'Troubles' up there have had at least one good side-effect. They've helped families to discover each other again.

'Have ye no homes to go to' used to be the usual adult rebuke to youngsters prowling the streets at night. No homes. Only houses. I think it's time we started building homes our children will be happy to stay in. We can't afford to rear them on the streets anymore like we used to.

A *terrible beauty*

She remembers vividly the night Thomas was born. How could she ever forget it! It was her husband who first told her the bad news. 'He is not fully normal,' he said, breaking it gently to her. And then the nurse carried him in and she saw for the first time the twisted little body. She went numb with shock and horror. 'It's not mine,' she kept repeating. 'Somebody has made a terrible mistake', and she turned towards the wall refusing even to look again at the baby. But there was no mistake. It was hers all right. And when she left the hospital a week later, Thomas came with her. It shames her now to remember what she thought then. And that was twelve years ago. Now last month Thomas died. And well-meaning friends say, 'It must be a great relief to her. Now she can really begin to live again.' But relief is not what she feels at all. She feels a huge, gaping emptiness in her life, the inconsolable grief of a mother who has just lost her child, her very own precious child.

It is incredible how much difference Thomas made in her life. Nobody could ever have told her before she had Thomas that she was the sort of woman who could cope so well with a badly handicapped child. She was a self-centred, selfish, slightly spoilt, pleasure-loving girl, and always was. Thomas, by his utter helplessness had brought out in her reserves of strength she never even thought she possessed. And look at Father! He was a gay, devil-may-care, good time charlie, when she first met him. People said they were well matched. Two of a kind. And now he was so different. A home-loving, family-man, deeply concerned about her and the children. And then the eldest boy, Michael. There was a gentleness, sensitiveness about him, quite untypical of his age. And the girls were a lot less selfish, a lot less spoilt. No doubt about it. Thomas had brought out the best in all of them and that simply by his cheerful uncomplaining presence, his unquestioning acceptance of the cruel limitations fate had imposed on him. In the words of the poem: they were 'all changed, changed utterly, a terrible beauty was born'. Thomas was their 'terrible beauty'.

They learned from Thomas what most of us may never learn. That the handicapped are special, very special people, God's own gentry in fact, because they change the very quality of our lives. As Thomas' family gratefully discovered, their handicaps make us more caring, more loving, more cheerful, and above all more grateful. They bring out the best in us. Without these crippled little witnesses we would all very soon degenerate into ungrateful and uncaring automatons. Like the shoeless begger, we never really realise how much we have to be thankful for until we meet the beggar with no legs. In a wonderfully strange way, it is the handicapped who contribute most towards making this a better world.

Inherit the wind

The little four-year-old boy had gone in under the table, sulking. He had been refused a second helping of ice-cream. His mother ordered him out, but the boy wouldn't budge. She tried coaxing. Nothing doing. Finally, she promised him the ice-cream, and he trotted out triumphantly and they both went out to the kitchen. There were two witnesses of this little domestic scene – grandmother and I. While the mother and son were being re-united in the kitchen over a dish of ice-cream, the old lady said to me. 'She isn't fair to the little lad; he doesn't know any better. She should have punished him.' I'd never heard it put that way before. Punishment as a service due to a child.

I remembered another similar incident.

I was visiting the home of a teacher when a woman called, and the teacher received her in the next room. I was embarrassed by the loud voices of what must have been a very stormy interview. The teacher, when the woman had left, felt he owed me an explanation. He hadn't promoted the women's son, because he couldn't read or write. If he passed on to the next grade, without knowing how to read or write, where reading and writing were presumed known and not specifically taught, there was a very real danger that the child would leave school and pass through life illiterate. The mother, over-sensitive to her child's disappointment and obsessed with what the neighbours might say or think, had tried to force the issue. 'For the boy's sake, I had to fight his own mother,' he said.

Life is full of similar experiences. There is the boy who wants to give up a subject . It's an attractive prospect for him – a free-period during school, less homework in the evening. He convinces his parents often surprisingly easily, that he is not able for the subject. In matters of education, parents whose own formal education ended with the primary school, are inclined to defer, too readily, to the opinions of their older children. And what of parents and teachers getting together to solve problems. Parents are often and mistakenly afraid to show their ignorance in educational matters to teachers. So it sometimes remains a conflict between student and teacher. What can the teacher do when a student insists on making a wrong decision?

The truth is he can do little more than advise or protest.

And why? It's a long story, going all the way back to the little boy under the table, looking for more ice-cream. Society, with its passion for oversimplification, for confusing authority with tyranny, punishment with excessive punishment, freedom with irresponsibility, has been so busy stripping adults of their authority, that they've unknowingly thrown out the baby with the bath water.

There is such a thing as moral authority whose purpose is to guide others to the goal of their life. And there is a grave obligation on the part of those responsible for the young to provide this moral authority where circumstances require it, where there is intellectual or moral defect in the dependant person or where that person is immature. A child's immaturity demands the service of this authority in order to mature. Where a parent or teacher fails to provide it, an injustice is done to the child, an injustice which may have long term effects on the child's life, the home and society. As the Bible puts it:

'He who misgoverns his house
inherits the wind.' (Prov. 11:29)

The family business

Take Johnny for example. He and his family live on High Street right in the public view. In his middle forties now, though he looks more like sixty. Very grey, a bit flabby. He's got eight children – in all sizes, from his eldest boy who has just finished his Leaving Cert to the baby still in diapers. Johnny runs a grocery-cum-haberdashery-cum-pub, and delivers milk and papers on the side. It's a family business. Everybody pitches in except the baby, and everybody takes his turn with both the baby and the shop. There's no great money in any side of it. But between the pub and the groceries, the milk and the newspapers, there's enough for Johnny and his family. But it's hard-earned. Work starts early – six o'clock. Each of the girls take it in turn to feed and change the baby. The oldest girl dresses the younger children for school. Johnny and the two younger boys load the crates of milk on the old station-wagon and set out on the milk-round. The older boy organises what's left of the labour-force for the paper round. And mother sets the table and prepares the breakfast. It's a tightly run schedule and when the 'flu strikes it's an emergency operation with those still on their feet doubling their work-load. Breakfast is a running buffet – each takes his own when they've completed their assignments. And then the exodus for school, never without its own crop of crises – pencils lost, copies missing, tears and tantrums. When they're all gone Johnny opens up the shop while mother washes up, does the rooms and starts the dinner. Even dinner is not a family meal. Somebody has to relieve Johnny in the shop while he gets his dinner. At about 3 o'clock the first of the bread-and-jam brigade begin to arrive and if it's fine they're sent out to play. But not for too long. There are still chores to be done. The boys clean the yard and cart the empties out of the shop. The girls get the tea and help with the washing-up. And everyone considered old enough, and that's nearly everyone, does a stint behind the counter. Then the homework for all, bed for the younger ones. Johnny and his wife do the bar. On busy nights the oldest boy and girl help out. It's pretty close to midnight when the last reluctant client is eased out, and another day is over. And so it continues, day after day with a little seasonal variation. Even on Sundays the shop has to be opened after Mass. Masses have to be staggered. And then the one and only break – Sunday afternoon. If it's fine they all pile into the station wagon and head for the sea. If it's wet, there's bedlam.

11

But Johnny is not complaining. Neither is his wife or family. They're lucky to be able to keep their doors open at all. Business is tricky. Overheads are high. Profits are small. Credit is scarce. Bad debts gobble up his profit. As Johnny says 'If somebody owes you money by the time he pays you, he's got the article at cost, and meanwhile you have to pay the interest on his loan.' And then there are the genuine hard-up cases. 'You can't turn your back on somebody you've known all your life when they're down on their luck.' So it's rarely he's not supporting some other family besides his own. And things are getting worse rather than better. The big singing-pubs are all the rage. He has to carry a wide variety of stock to cater for all tastes. 'These young ones want very fancy drinks.' And the grocery trade is even in bigger trouble. Supermarkets are springing up all over the place. And the small men are being squeezed out. Johnny is holding the devil by the tail and he knows it. As he has it figured, if he can keep his doors open long enough to educate his family and see them all started there will always be enough in it for himself and the wife at the latter end. 'After that the devil can take it.'

But he's got his invisible assests and he knows it. Even though it doesn't show up in his Profit and Loss Account. It's what makes the whole venture a thriving concern, instead of an exercise in survival. Because Johnny's aim in life is not to make money but to make a home. He may not have much of a business but he's got a fine family and a wonderful home. His children may well come up in the world; get white-collared jobs with regular hours; have fewer children. But when it comes to making a home their ideal will always be that shop on High Street. A family business that made the family its business.

Lost and found

It was one of those beautiful Summer days. And I decided to head for the beach. I decided to stop at this house I know and bring the family with me. It would be a big treat for them. There was a young mother and her four little toddlers. The husband was away at work. They were thrilled at the idea. So we all piled in and made for the sea. When we got there I deposited the mother and her toddlers on the strand and promised to collect them again about tea-time. I found a nice secluded spot in the sandhills for myself and I settled into it for the afternoon.

I'm not quite sure when I became conscious that something was wrong. It must have been about two hours later. I began to notice a fairly persistent trickle of people passing the spot where I was sun-bathing. Finally I stopped one of them and asked what was all the activity about. 'There's a little child lost,' he said. My God! I knew instantly. It had to be one of my protegés. I rushed back to where I had left the mother. And sure enough, she was in a state of near-hysteria. Little Eileen, the two-and-a-half year old, was missing.

I'll never forget the next few hours. Fear gripped my stomach like a vice. It was all my fault. It was I who had suggested the trip. And their father didn't even know about it. We searched everywhere but no sign of Eileen. People are awfully good in a situation like that. Everybody joined in the search. Perfect strangers gave up their evening to help find her. We tried to figure out how far a two and a half year old child could walk. We combed the sandhills for miles around. And then there were other horrible possibilities that had to be faced. The tide had come in in the meantime. Was she drowned? She couldn't be, we convinced ourselves desperately. She was afraid of the water. Maybe she had headed uptown? Or was hit by a car? I went to the barracks. An old guard came back with me. They had reports recently of some unsavoury character prowling in the sandhills and interfering with little children.

Finally, in sheer desperation I climbed the highest sandhill and scanned the area for miles around. I saw a speck in the distance. Could have been a towel or a pair of togs. I looked and looked but it didn't move. But it was something. Without taking my eyes off it I made for the spot. Sure enough it was little Eileen, lying face downwards, asleep. It must have been every bit of three miles away.

Coming home in the car, I noticed how the mother – she was

sitting in front holding the baby—used to turn around every so often to look at Eileen who was curled up in the back seat fast asleep. The others didn't exist just then. She had eyes for nobody else. Eileen, by being lost, had become special. Like the Prodigal Son and the Good Thief and Mary Magdalen. Like the alcoholic who gets off it or the drug-addict who makes it back or the criminal who goes straight. Or like any other one of the host of unfortunate creatures who go through hell and find their way back. Like Eileen, they had become special in the eyes of God.

Santa Claus

Christmas is coming and the geese are getting fat,
Please put a penny in the poor man's hat.
If you haven't got a penny, a half-penny will do.
If you haven't got a half-penny, God bless you.

That little rhyme, more than anything else, brings me back to the Christmases of my childhood. I can remember my mother in the kitchen making the plum-pudding, and the porter-cake and the stuffing for the turkey. And there were things I didn't like too – plucking the turkey was one of them and I always seemed to have been landed with that job. But there was a great feeling of excitement and anticipation the week before Christmas – at least until I stopped believing in Santa Claus. I could have killed that older boy in our street who first told me there was no Santa.

Why *I* should have wanted to defend Santa so much, is now beyond me. I never got anything very fabulous off him – at least by today's standards. As far as I can remember now, it was always something ordinary like socks or handkerchiefs, knitted gloves or a scarf with the odd game thrown in, like draughts or ludo or snakes-and-ladders. I can remember too a box of water-colours, a mouth-organ and a torch which was very handy for bringing in the turf from the shed at night. . . I can't honestly remember anything else now but I do remember they gave me an awful lot of pleasure then.

Looking round the big city stores now, I notice that Santa has really hit the big-time since I was a child. The sheer range, the sophistication of modern toys is staggering. And in a way I feel sorry for children today. They have only to look in the nearest shop-window to see there a hundred good reasons for being dissatisfied with whatever they get. And I sympathise with parents too. One has only to look at the sophistication of modern toys to see that the toy-market is aimed at the parents rather than the children. Children now, as children always, are easily pleased. Mercifully, they are not price-tag conscious. How often have you noticed that it's the simple cheap toy, like the old rag-doll, that they love most. We should preserve this innocence of theirs and protect them as long as possible from commercial exploitation. Besides, it's a mistake to give children early in life expensive tastes and great expectations.

If you are tempted to make a big splash for your child this Christmas, it might be a good thing to remind yourself that you won't always

15

be there to play Santa Claus for him. Life is no Christmas and modern society is certainly no Santa Claus. Parents like politicians shouldn't make their children promises they can't hope to keep. The presents you give them this Christmas might someday become the grudges of an 18-year-old, for whom society can only offer a place in a dole-queue.

The great consumer

Children seem to be nearly always eating. Ice-cream, lollipops, crisps, sweets. Going to school, coming from school and in school I imagine too. An AD-man's dream come true – non-stop consumers. An endless flow of pennies to build the great corporations. And happy, smiling, eating, chewing faces of a vast army of children.

'Give me your children and you can have the adults.' Is this what we are doing? Are we giving away our children? And why? For a little bit of peace and quiet. To get them out from under our feet: to give us a chance to cope.

What harm is there in a few little sweets? There might be none. Ask the mother of an alcoholic or drug addict or sex-maniac. Ask the parents of a little girl who was spirited away in a car by a strange man with a few sweets and all because she had never learned to say no. If these parents had their lives to live over again, they might do things differently.

But apart from all this, what is going to happen to you when you can no longer supply their demands, when their other appetites have been aroused? And what is going to happen to you when you begin to make demands on them? 'Really, Mother, I'd help if I could, but I've got my own life to live now.' Or simply: 'I'll write, Mother.' 'Chin up, Dad, I'll keep in touch.' Will all this glorious summer of parents and children peter out into a Christmas-card connection? And is this all inevitable?

'The hand that rocks the cradle shakes the world.' Whatever is going to happen in the future is happening now in the home. Babies that are picked up every time they cry now, may be the street-protesters of tomorrow. Babies don't have to be shown how to grasp with both hands – their instincts tell them that. But they have to be shown how to let go. And this is a painful and noisy process. The instant tantrum that jangles every nerve in your system. Keep a sweet handy if you want instant peace.

But instant tantrums – instant sweets may be corruption – not correction. It may be the first lesson of a street-protester, wildcat striker, of an anarchist or agitator. It may be that it was here, in the cradle, they first learned that it was not the meek, as Christ said, but those who shout loudest who will inherit the earth.

Take the time and trouble to teach your child how to say no and you will have started a Christian. And if you have taught your child to say no you have nothing to fear in this big bad world of ours. Because it has no hidden traps. For those who can say no it holds no terrors.

Too late, Dr Spock

Dr Spock had a theory that the best way to rear children was to let them do whatever they wanted to do. The devil, according to Dr Spock, was repression. Repressed children became unhappy adults. So down with authoritarianism – in the home, in the schools, in religion, in society. Children should be permitted to do whatever they liked. Dr Spock was one of the fathers of what became known as the permissive society.

It was a very attractive theory. Especially to a generation of parents whose own childhood was spent under the shadow of a somewhat grim authoritarianism. They were the days when children should be seen but not heard. And punishment was a regular feature of daily life at home as well as in school. So Dr Spock found an eager audience for his theory. A whole generation of parents, especially in America, accepted it as gospel and reared their children accordingly. And so America, as somebody once said, became the 'first country in the world where parents were completely obedient to their children'.

But inevitably, time passed, the Spock babies grew up into the Spock teenagers of the sixties, and later the Spock adults of the seventies and eighties. And lo, and behold, they weren't any happier or any better adjusted than the previous generation. If anything, a heck of a lot less. In fact, some became drop-outs, hippies, drug-addicts. Others swelled the growing numbers of young alcoholics. The 'brave new world' did not materialise.

In the early seventies, Dr Spock decided to revise his theory. He surveyed, coldly and clinically, as always, the society his theory had helped in no small measure to create. Good scientist that he was, he did not hesitate to admit its shortcomings. And where did he go wrong? By attempting above all to replace parents with experts. Rearing children is the last important area in life still left largely in the hands of amateurs. And thank God for that. When parents go wrong in bringing up their children they may, at the very worst, add a couple of delinquent children to the world. When experts make mistakes, they may produce a delinquent world. As one commentator put it: 'It's too late, Dr Spock.'

Discos

The morning after he looks anything but good. And how could he? After four hours sleep? When you're fifteen and burning up all that energy you need your sleep – every minute of it. He sits in the front seat of the class. An old man's face on a young pair of shoulders. He was at the disco last night. He averages almost three a week. On a quiet night he never gets to bed before twelve. On a disco-night it's pretty late. You see, around here, travelling to discos is the norm rather than the exception. Twenty miles is not regarded as excessive. And anyhow, the local hall sort of cramps his style. He can fairly let his hair down in the anonymity of a neighbouring parish. And since he started having a jar or two before the disco, it's safer out-of-town. 'You're not likely to run into some nosey busybody, eager to split on you to the "oul fella". What he doesn't know won't bother him.' By the time the crowd are rounded up after the disco it's pretty late. Some of the guys are inclined to do a bit of messing around after the disco and more often than not he's one of them. And all that smoking! He can get through a large packet without any bother between home and back. He has to bum a cigarette the following morning during the break – as he puts it – to restore his shattered nerves.

Adults are inclined to view the whole youth scene as a result of a more general permissiveness. But permissiveness is a blanket-term. It's a description of the state of things rather than the cause of them. I'm inclined to think that money is the key factor. 'Money is the root of all evil!' I don't think we ever take it quite seriously enough. Probably the main reason why I didn't live it up like a 15-year-old today was simply because I didn't have the money. And even if my parents were tempted to spoil me, they couldn't because they didn't have the money. Canned entertainment for youth was simply not there because there was no market for it. No money in it. If I had to get parental permission for every time I stepped outside the door – and I did – perhaps it was because I had to ask for the money. I can remember well when fourpence for the pictures was a big deal. The old days were lean times. And if they now appear to have been more virtuous days, too, maybe the shortage of money was a large part of the reason. Very often the difference between going wrong or keeping right is opportunity not virtue. Money provides an awful lot of opportunities. It opens a lot of doors. And money can buy a lot of trouble. A 15-year-old today has easy access to the sort of money I didn't even dream

20

about when I was his age. Small wonder he has acquired expensive habits, some of which he can't cope with because he's not mature enough. If you give him money or allow him to keep what he comes by, you might not really be doing him a favour. With money in his pocket he's a marked man, a prime target for exploitation. If you really want to help Junior with his problems, you can make a start by freezing his assets. As long as you control each item on his expense account, at least you'll know what he's up to.

A job for junior

'Sure, it keeps him out of trouble, Father,' his mother tells you. 'It'll make a man of him,' Father says, bursting with pride when he tells you how much the young lad is making. Junior is a school-boy in his early teens and he has just landed his first summer-job. The whole family looks up to the new man in the house, the new breadwinner. It seems to be a pretty well-established practice now.

There are advantages and in some homes where things are difficult it is a real blessing. But there is a debit side too. And it is far too important not to face up to. Quite a sizeable number of teenagers stay in boarding-schools for eight months of the year. If they get a job during the holidays – and many leave home, some even the country for these jobs – then for all practical purposes they are finished with home. Or more importantly, home is finished with them. Some parents cease to play a really big part in the rearing of their children after they reach the age of twelve or thirteen simply because they don't see very much of them after that age.

If you encourage your little boy to get a job, you shouldn't be all that surprised if he is not your little boy anymore. You're putting him in the big league. He will be spending most of his time with the men now. Sharing their work-benches and their lunch-breaks and – let's face it – their adult jokes too. They will be his finishing school. They will take over where you left off. You may have abandoned him before he is fully fledged. So don't blame them if you are disappointed with the finished product.

You may be giving him, at a fairly tender age, the only real independence that counts in this world – financial independence. It is amazing the difference that makes to your relationship with him. While you held the purse-strings, you had the last word. You may well be hurt when he doesn't defer to your wishes any more, but you should not really be surprised. It is his own money. He can do with it what he likes. It may not be what you like. As for learning the value of money! He gets his board and lodgings completely free, from you. His education and clothes are taken care of. He has no commitments. Some parents think it is not right to ask Junior for a contribution towards his keep. He will be a long time earning his living before he has that sort of spare cash again. Small wonder some of the young wage-earners are strike-happy.

In later life, he probably won't thank you for having given him his wings so early. He will be more conscious then of what he has lost – his boyhood years. That time in a boy's life when sport is a passion, when he is keen to face challenges and learns to accept triumph and disaster on the playing field. That time when he trains his mind and limbs to work together for a single purpose, when he has to rely on friends and work as part of a team. That time too, when he comes to know his limitations and accepts them, when he acquires skills and interests that will carry him through many a bleak period in later life. Instead Junior is learning how to drink his first pint and doss on his first job.

The Bible puts it succinctly:

There is a season for everything,
A time for every occupation under heaven.
A time for giving birth,
A time for dying. . . (Eccles 3:1-2)

There is a time in life to be a man and a time too to be a boy.

Mother knows best

Looking back at it now you wonder what all the trouble was about. And there was trouble. A cloud of gloom had descended over the whole family. The tension was almost unbearable. Rows flared up at the drop of a hat. And people were forever storming out of the house, banging doors after them. Everybody's nerves were on edge. It all started the day Maureen marched in and announced she was getting engaged. It seems that her fiancé didn't quite measure up. Mother took it worst and Father, though I suspect he wasn't all that disturbed at the prospect, backed up Mother. The rest of the family were split down the middle – the younger ones generally all for Maureen and the older ones against. The fiery scenes quickly gave way to a new phase – silence. And that was the worst time when Mother and Maureen stopped talking. And for the rest, it became the great unmentionable subject. In fact, things got so bad Maureen decided to leave home and go into digs. But the opposition only increased her determination. She got engaged and a date was set for the marriage. It was then Mother started her Novenas and getting Masses said for a 'very special intention'. There was even some talk for a while about her making a trip to Lourdes. It was sad meeting Maureen in the street. She looked so strained and so determined. As the wedding day approached there was even talk of the family not attending. But in the end, as they say 'wiser counsels prevailed' and they went. But it was a very strained affair.

Well, it's all over now, thank God. Mother is crazy about her two little grand-children. She can't see enough of them. As for her son-in-law, she is quite fond of him really. Well, she never had anything against him personally except his job and his background. Mind you, she is still conscious of it. She speaks of him to the neighbours as being 'a very important man in his firm, a sort of manager'. She has changed tactics in her prayers too. They are mainly directed now towards his promotion.

The whole thing puts me in mind of a phenomenon which occurs frequently in rural parts. Sometimes when you're driving along in the evening you meet a man bringing his cows home. Balancing a bicycle on one hand and brandishing a stick on the other he eventually herds the cattle to one side to make it possible for you to pass. And so you would too, if only he himself would get out of the way. You could have edged your way past the cattle much easier if there was no one with them. I sometimes think it must be the sort of experience God suffers most from. Those with the best intentions must often cause him the most bother.

Bachelor husbands

She never guessed it was going to be like this. And when you think of their courtship days! He couldn't keep away from her – ringing her up at the office, bumping into her during the lunch-break, dropping into the flat in the evenings. She used to have quite a job trying to get him to go home at night. And her poor flat-mate ready to collapse with sleep, making frantic eyes at her. Sharing the one bed-sitter she couldn't go to bed until he left. He seemed to have only one almighty interest then and that was her. And he resented everybody and everything that took her away from him. Her job, her girl-friends. He was barely civil to her flat-mate. He thought she was a bit soured because she had no boy of her own. She could never figure out what he used to do before he met her. He took a drink but didn't seem particularly drawn to the pub unless she suggested it. He took a mild interest in inter-county football but the nearest they ever came to a football match was watching the All-Ireland on T.V. She knew he had a bag of golf-clubs in the boot of the car but she never saw him take them out.

In the first year of their marriage he was still very attentive. They went everywhere together. More often than not he was perfectly happy to sit at home as long as she was there. And then things began to change – so gradual at first that she didn't even notice it. He began to slip out occasionally to the pub to meet a crowd of the lads. An odd Saturday he had a four-ball lined up. And an odd Sunday he took off for a football match. In fact she was quite pleased to see him go out at first. It gave her a chance to get a few things done. But very quickly he began to refind his old life – the one she didn't even know existed. Golf every evening and all Saturday; travelling to matches every Sunday, pub every night. He didn't even seem to have time to cut the lawn any more. And there were handles falling off doors, windows that wouldn't close and the bathroom closet was leaning out from the wall like the Tower of Pisa. Now, they hardly ever go out together except perhaps to a friend's wedding or a relative's funeral. She's just another disillusioned wife. She is married to a bachelor. She feeds her husband and washes his clothes. And he pay the bills. They still share the same bed and the same table. That is about as much as is left of what once promised to be a wonderful marriage.

Theirs is a marriage which is far more common than we care to believe. And while there is no justification for a bachelor-husband, there are some things the unfortunate wife should not do. Nagging is a mistake, not because she isn't fully entitled to nag but because her husband will jump at it as an excuse for neglecting her even more. And then such a drastic change in a husband's behaviour requires some explanation. It is at least possible that she too may have changed after marriage. Girls who were gay and attractive before marriage sometimes let themselves become very dowdy and domineering very soon afterwards. He may have been the first to become disillusioned. But above all, the children should not be used as pawns. You can't compensate for a neglecting husband by spoiling your child. You can't feed your baby on the resentment you feel towards its father. Very often the only real loser in these marriages are the children. And that's the one reason you must keep trying to salvage your marriage. It will mean putting up with an awful lot of foul play, resisting some terrible provocation, swallowing an awful lot of pride. But you owe it to your children to keep trying. Above all you owe it to your husband – the man you once fell in love with. You may be his only real hope of salvation.

Remember the words you chose to be read at your wedding:

Love bears all things, believes all things,
hopes all things, endures all things. (1 Cor 13:7)

A life of her own

She was the centre of attraction. All eyes were on her. And everybody said she was such a beautiful bride. And so she was. The wedding album is still there to prove it. Ironically her wedding day was to be the last time that she occupied the centre of the stage. She seems to shift further and further into the background as time goes by. She looks at her wedding photos now, somewhat like the donkey in the poem remembers Palm Sunday. 'I, also, had my hour, one far fierce hour and sweet.' There are times when she thinks that the donkey and herself have more in common than that one glorious hour.

And yet she herself would be the first to admit that hers is not a bad marriage by any stretch of the imagination. There are many married women who envy her – her fine home, her adoring husband, her beautiful children. She gets out of the house fairly regularly – though always with the family. They go for a drive on Sundays – at least on the Sundays there isn't any football match her husband particularly wants to see. They take a house for a few weeks every year at the sea-side. And she comes back as brown as if she had been to the Costa Brava. She even manages a few dinner-dances – those her husband is expected to attend and bring his wife. She usually spends them chatting with a few other abandoned wives while their husbands settle world affairs at the bar.

And when you add to that the ICA meetings, the occasional parent-teacher meeting, the sewing class and of course the shopping, not to forget the Sunday Mass and the annual mission, there are many who would think she has a very busy social life.

As they say, 'She has a lot to be thankful for.' When you think of the poor unfortunate wives of alcoholics, the deserted wives, the battered wives. Or the wives of mean husbands. Husbands who watch every penny or worse still do all the shopping themselves. Or those who are the mothers of a handicapped child. Or single mothers. When you list them like that, she has indeed a lot to be thankful for. And I suppose that is why she never complains. If she did, people might think she was becoming neurotic.

All the same she can't help feeling deprived. She too would like a 'life of her own', something even her children are very insistent on for themselves. Something her husband takes for granted as his due. Is it so terrible for her to want a life of her own too? Why should wives and mothers be expected to make all the sacrifices – even though

28

they gladly do, and always will.

Men could give their wives a little more of their rights by giving up some of their own privileges. They could insist and in most cases, they would have to insist, on them getting out and making a life of their own. And of course, stay at home a little oftener themselves, and who knows, they might even begin a beautiful friendship with those other little strangers they helped bring into this world.

Getting Out of the Way

One way or another, the world is full of drivers other than motorists. Wives drive their husbands. The reverse is equally true though much less acknowledged. Parents drive their children, as children do their parents, though not always consciously. Teachers drive their pupils who return the complement by driving them mad. Employers drive employees relentlessly; unions drive management to near despair. In the practice of driving others, very few can justly claim to be more sinned against than sinning. Most of it comes under the heading of interfering; all of it is intended for somebody else's good. No good ever comes from it. How often it happens that adolescent or young adults abandon their religion because their parents shoved it down their throats. Or their religious teachers left them with a distaste that outlived their catechesis. 'Give me the child and you can have the man,' the Jesuits used to say. But that was before James Joyce. And unfortunately, in these times, Joyce is not the near solitary exception he used to be.

Christ said: 'I am the Way,' and if we removed the obstacles of ourselves, many would find the Way. The word of God, unhindered and uncompromised by our dishonesty, is powerfully attractive. More miracles of grace are probably bungled by somebody blundering into another's life than we realise. We should be vessels of mercy, channels of grace, for those in our lives and in our care. Too often, we are great bloody clots blocking the arteries of God's grace. 'I must become less and less,' John said, 'so that he can become more and more.' Not a bad motto that, for parents and teachers, no less than bishops and politicians. But then John was unique. He not only preached 'Make way for the Lord', he practised it by getting out of the way when the Lord came. His uniqueness was that he knew exactly the moment when he was no longer needed. When to bow out. History had no precedents for such extraordinary behaviour. Imagine a Fidel Castro as he rides triumphantly into Havana on the wings of a successful revolution, slipping away quietly into oblivion. Or a Charles de Gaulle, as he led the Allies down the Champs Elysées at the Liberation of Paris, sneaking back meekly into private life. Men do, of course, retire. When they are old and tired and past their best. When people are beginning to notice their mistakes and comment on them. When they are hard-pressed by young Turks, eager to go places. And even then for most of them it isn't easy. Notice how painfully even prelates are parted from their privileges and power.

But John the Baptist was young, in his prime, with the world at his feet. 'Behold the Lamb of God.' The moment he chose to bow out is marvellously immortalised in the Mass – just before Communion. If Christ is to find a cradle in the hearts of others at Christmas, perhaps we too should bow out and leave some room there for him.

HOME

Unwanted mothers

She never thought it would come to this. In fact she never thought about it at all. She never had time. With six children to rear and an over-worked husband to worry about, wondering about her own future was simply a luxury she couldn't afford. Life was just one continuous series of crises then. If it wasn't baby falling out of the pram, it was his big brother in trouble at school or their father under pressure at his job. And there was nearly always one of them in bed, down with something or other. As she used to say then, if there was anything going around one of her lot were bound to catch it. As they grew up things grew worse rather than better. Their problems seemed to grow bigger with them or at least they weren't the sort any more that a mother could really solve. But they all brought them to her anyway and she did their worrying for them. And then the endless bickering between them. She was their only court of appeal. Father was not to be bothered.

And then it all changed so rapidly. Within a couple of years in fact. The children left one by one in quick succession for jobs and getting them all placed wasn't easy. But they managed it somehow. And then there was only Joan left and she was as much trouble as the whole lot put together – threatening even for a while to drop out. But she straightened herself out in time. Then the marriages started. For a while the problems and the excitement were greater than ever. Then Father retired and at last they seemed all set for a long spell of peace and quiet – their well-earned rest. But it was not to be. Father finally succumbed to all the pressures that had accumulated over the years. A coronary took him away suddenly in his late sixties.

And now she is completely alone. It was about the only problem that her life had left her totally unprepared for. All her life was spent looking after others. She was completely unequipped to look after herself. And time which she never had enough of to do all she had to do, was her biggest burden now. If only she had somebody to do something for. He family didn't need her anymore. But how she needed them! To worry about them, to advise them, to mother them. Above all help them rear her grandchildren. But unfortunately for her that is known as interference nowadays. And maybe it is. One hears a lot nowadays about unmarried mothers and unwanted babies. But one hears very little about what I think is at least numerically a far greater problem, and that is the unwanted mother. The mother

32

who has reared her family and is abandoned. I honestly don't know what the answer is. But one thing is certain. Nobody and least of all mothers should be left to end their days alone, deprived of the one thing that made sense of their lives. Other people to worry about.

School

School report

Tommy is stupid. That is not putting it nicely, and certainly it will have to be phrased differently to his mother. That is the problem. Tommy's teacher has to fill in his school-report or, at least, the two lines allotted to the subject. What can he say, in two lines, about Tommy that is truthful and useful but not hurtful? There are other nicer phrases of course. Every teacher has a pocketful of them and each has his own preferences; low IQ, intellectually weak, has a problem, unresponsive, slow, etc. But with or without the sugar-coating, the pill is hard to swallow for Tommy's mother.

For Tommy's sake and her own, swallow it she must. And yet she will grasp at every straw in the wind rather than face the facts. It's the teacher's fault – he doesn't really know Tommy, doesn't understand him, or doesn't know his job. Takes no interest in his pupils. Or it's Tommy fault – doesn't do his lessons, too fond of football or knocks around with the wrong crowd. Or even, it's her own fault – I should spend more time helping with his homework, I'm always taking him away from his books, I let him watch too much TV. Granted, all these are good and valid reasons and they do make a difference to his progress. But the difference is marginal. The truth is that this boy has a low IQ and what aggravates the problem is that his mother attaches too much importance to academic ability and, without meaning to, makes life harder for her son by coaxing, goading, pushing him beyond what he is capable of. Strange, isn't it, that mothers can accept that their sons are poor at sports or that their daughters are plain but not that their children are intellectually weak. And don't be misled by those who openly confess it to all and sundry. *They* might say it but *you* daren't.

School is, in fact, a discrimination machine (and so, for that matter, is life. Footballers are chosen for their height; fashion-models for their looks.) School discriminates among pupils on the basis of intellectual ability. And it's hard, very hard, on the weaker ones. It is a system of education and like any system, it has its limitations, and its faults. It is designed to cater for the masses and it confines itself almost exclusively to intellectual formation. Within these limits, it is reasonably efficient. On the other hand, its faults are largely the faults of the individuals who work the system and those for whom it is worked. Teachers, very often unconsciously, may overemphasise the importance of intellectual ability and this obsession is invariably passed on to the pupils. But more important still is the attitude of the parents. If they expect too much from their children, they may do them great harm. Children want so much to please their parents.

Life is full of failures, – people who couldn't live up to the expectations of their parents. They failed because their parents set too high standards for them and they tried to hard to reach them. Education in a very real sense is getting to know one's limitations and learning to live with them.

Tommy is a *person* not an IQ specimen, and during his schooldays he needs to be reminded of this. And who better than his mother to do this. He is cheerful and kind, honest and humble. A good tryer and a good mixer. On balance, the human race is very lucky to have him. Above all, he is a creature of God, a masterpiece in his own right. God loves him, not in spite of, but rather because of his poor intelligence. In God's eyes, there is no room for radical improvement. In the end, nothing else matters.

Mercator's Projection

Mercator's Projection used to figure periodically on examination papers in my school days. Mercator was a Dutch cartographer who attempted to reproduce the earth which is round and three-dimensional on a piece of paper which is rectangular and two-dimensional. The result was the projection named after him and a dubious immortality among students of geography. The attempt was not completely successful but it does serve certain uses, notably for navigators.

It reminds one of examinations themselves which attempt to reduce a person who is complex and multidimensional to an examination paper which is narrow and selective and two-dimensional. It is impossible but the exercise can be useful. Exams, at best, are a very feeble attempt at classifying people within a very restricted area, a poor enough method of cataloguing school-leavers to facilitate their transfer into the available job-slots. Even on this basis, it is not highly successful. A casual observer of life can see that there are a sizeable number of square pegs in round holes. If job satisfaction is the criterion of success, then exams have a lot to answer for.

Year after year, school-leaving classes are classified by their exams, from the first to the last. Twenty years later, it would not be unduly surprising to find that life's assessment of this same group shows them in exactly the reverse order. Those who regularly attend Past Pupils' Unions can vouch for that. Somebody there can be overheard remarking to his wife, 'See that fellow over there. At school he could hardly spell his name. Look at him now. He could buy the whole school out of his loose change.' Those who come last in their exams may well turn out best in later life. Or perhaps the most happily married, the most successful in coping with life in general. What the exam paper does *not* record is much, much more important than what it does.

In fairness to the exam system, it doesn't make any exaggerated claims. But society very often does. It is understandable that universities and other third level institutions insist on certain grades as a minimum requirement for entrants. Why business and other professions do is not so clear. A form of snobbery, perhaps? Insisting on high grades for low professions has become almost standard practice at present with the job shortage. It helps to reduce drastically the number of applicants and spare the management the time consumed by interviews. Employers who succumb to this temptation are the real losers. No enterprise, private or public, can afford to turn up its nose at honesty, a scarce commodity in all occupations. Well big business knows this when it has to budget against losses through pilfering and fiddled expense accounts by employees. The steady, honest, reliable person is an asset in any company. No examination yet devised awards a certificate of honesty or reliability. These are awarded only posthumously in the final examination we will all have to take. The results will be declared for all to hear:

Well done, good and faithful servant;
You have been faithful over a little, I will set you over much:
Enter into the joy of your master. (Mt 25:21)

The class genius

I remember one schoolmate in particular, the class genius. Teachers doted on him and their admiration rubbed off on us. He was top of the class at everything, sailed through his exams with flying colours. It was no surprise to us when he waltzed through his final exam, scooping up a fistful of A's or B's to earn himself a university scholarship. The world was at his feet. Nobody doubted then but that he was destined for a brilliant career.

That was the last I saw or heard of him for over twenty years until I ran into him recently. I had a job to conceal my surprise when finally I recognised him. It wasn't that he was down and out – far from it – but you could tell at a glance that he wasn't on top any more, and hadn't been there for a long time. He tried so hard to explain what had happened to him, how everybody had conspired again him. He mustn't have cornered as good a listener for a long time, he whined so much that night. To listen was the least that I could do. I owed that much to the memory of what he once was. If only you knew him when I knew him. If you knew how far ahead he was at the start in the line of brains and opportunities, you couldn't help but feel there was a breach of promise somewhere. I don't really know whether I was sorry for him, or sickened by him.

What happened to him? It is a long story, at least the way he told it to me. You would have to fish very carefully for it in the torrent of prejudices, rash judgements, condemnations, grudges, excuses, etc, etc, that poured out of him. The sort of talk that is heavily laced with phrases like, 'but I was too smart for them', 'they thought they could fix me', 'I'm no flat, nobody is going to pull a fast one on me'. The irony of them was so patent. It was knowing the singer that made the song so sad.

It seems he was fond of the drink but in fairness I think that was the end rather than the beginning of the story, the effect rather than the cause. Drink often fills the gap left by unrealised ambitions. There were three or four bosses he didn't get on very well with. Their fault, of course, all four of them. Things weren't any better with his own staff. 'An incompetent lot' according to him. He didn't suffer fools very easily and, unwisely, he didn't always distinguish between those who were above him and those who were below him. Inevitably, the latter suffered most. The Union had to intevene over one alleged assault he made on a junior. 'I just boxed his ears,' he said, as if it was the most natural way in the world to treat a fumbling subordinate. He didn't talk much about his home life except to say, 'she fooled me into it before I realised what I was doing.' That was enough to indicate the present sad state of that union. He certainly had his problems but to listen to him talk, he could set the whole world right, given half a chance.

Where did he go wrong? It is possible he thought he could master all problems with the same ease that he mastered those on exam papers. By the time he had finished university he was eighteen years at school. All that time he was on top of his world, a world of Latin sentences, French compositions and mathematical problems. All these years he basked in the sunshine of teachers' favour. There is something akin to a love-affair between brilliant pupils and their teachers. And he fairly lapped up the admiration of the rest of us. Remember how easy it was to curry favour with the class genius, simply by telling him how great he was. With all his brains, he was very innocent. He didn't have to study people as hard as the rest of us had, just to survive. He studied books instead. But you can't handle other people like a piece of French syntax or a mathematical equation. And the trouble in life is other people. Sadly, the world for him is peopled with demons, all out to get him. And all his brains are more a hindrance than a help to him now.

Day dreams

Did you ever wonder what you might have become if only things had been different when you were a child. The world might have lost a great pianist just because your family couldn't afford piano lessons when you were young, or a great athlete if only you had been spotted in time. There are moments in our lives when we imagine we hear the thunderous applause of the concert hall or the roar of a crowd in a stadium, thousands leaping to their feet in recognition of our unique talents. Flights of fancy, that help to compensate for the dullness of the daily routine. Inside every small man, they say, there's a tall one trying to break out.

There are other illusions much more dangerous because so little different from reality it is easy to believe in them. Things might easily have turned out that way. A chance taken here, an opportunity seized there, a bit of a push once in a while, a bit of help or guidance at the right moment, a little more understanding and I could have made it. I could be where my boss is today. Dangerous fantasies these. Dangerous for you beause they leave a bitterness, a feeling of frustration, a chip on your shoulder. And unfortunate for others. A wife who has to carry the burden of them, and children who have to grow up with them, and be driven to succeed where their parents had failed. The man who couldn't make the county team himself compensated eventually by having his son make it.

The winter of discontent in life has its spring sowing. The day-dreams of the class-room may have a sinister side. It mattered little at the time if their only loss was the conjugation of a Latin verb or the causes of the Thirty Years' War. Life has a nasty habit of settling outstanding accounts later, much later. The classroom desk may have been the cradle of middle-aged disillusionment. 'Dreams give wings to fools', the Bible says, and dreams inevitably end in disillusionment.

There are many influences on a growing boy and school is only one of them. Though, in many respects, it is a very sheltered existence, it is the first outside world a child meets after leaving home. It provides the environment in which he can develop the qualities he will need in later life – tolerance, friendship, enthusiasm, ambition, persistence. At eighteen he should have a fair idea of what life is really like and of his own ability to cope with it. If he hasn't, he has missed the whole point of education. He may be setting out on a road that leads only to disillusionment.

Every pub in the country has its share of such people among its clientele, and there is no barman who hasn't acted father-confessor to this type of individual on occasion. We can all spot them a mile away. This is their real tragedy. Everybody knows them except themselves. No one can tell them because they don't want to believe it. They are schoolboys who never grew up. Dreamers who never really woke up. They limp through life, looking for recognition, on the basis of what might have been. The world is hard, but in its own way, fair. It pays for goods delivered. They want their payment on credit. It is a pity they won't acccept themselves for what they're really worth – no small thing in the sight of God. It is a pity they never learned from the poet who said:

> If you can dream – and not make dreams your master
> Yours is the Earth and everything that's in it
> And – which is more – you'll be a Man, my son.

The class photo

Occasionally in later life, something comes up in conversation which recalls our schooldays. Invariably, somebody says, 'Do you remember so-and-so? I wonder what became of him.' I suppose, in all, we remember about a half a dozen or so of our classmates, the class genius, the best footballer, the funny guy and one or two special friends from the days of special friendships. The others have disappeared. If somebody produces a class-photo we would probably recall their names, but that is about all we can remember about them now. By our standards then, they were mediocre and by exam standards even less than mediocre. Yet they sat with us for five years in the same class-room, laughed at the same jokes from teachers with the same, 'counterfeited glee', carried the same burdens except much more of them. In the end, to nobody's great surprise, they left, labelled E or F. School and they parted, mutually relieved, though it contrived to leave them in no doubt that they had let down a fine institution.

What became of them? Classified ads provide no space for Es and Fs. Modern business has a prejudice against losers. While educationalists may have succeeded in substituting grades E and F for the category failure, the improvement is little more than cosmetic. They are still stigmatised in the eyes of employers and interviewers. Worse still, they may well be psychologically scarred. The first hurdle for them is the hardest. But they enjoy one enormous advantage. There is only one direction they can go and that is up.

What they lacked by way of intelligence, they have more than gained by way of experience. They have learned the only really important lessons which only their sort of experience can teach. They have been schooled in adversity, the best of all life's teachers. Not one single moment of their schooldays has been wasted, whatever the record may show. The long hours struggling with problems they could never hope to solve, the desperate attempts to conceal an ignorance that was all too obvious, the torment of a long day whose only friendly sound was that of a bell, the humiliations, the harsh words of teachers and worst of all, the titters of classmates. There is no certificate to record all this but nobody can be called a failure who has endured it all and survived.

There are casualties, of course. Some are crushed by a system Patrick Pearse once called 'the murder-machine'. They are probably not as numerous as he and others would have us believe. Young people have a remarkable talent for surviving. In spite of the Classified ads, those whom school labelled failures do find a niche for themselves in life. And they are happy because if they have learned nothing else in school, they have learned to be grateful for small favours. The appreciation denied them in school they get in good measure afterwards from wives who love them, children who worship them and friends who value them. Above all, they are humble as only those are humble who have been often humiliated. Of all the virtues that grace humanity, humility is probably the most attractive. It is an enormous asset for those who share their lives with others. Their success in life is assured. They have Christ's own word for it:

Happy are the meek, for they shall inherit the earth. (Mt 5:5)

Those whom the gods love

It was a strange experience to stand on the sideline and watch him play. He played his heart out. This was a very important match for him. Teddy was going on 18 and this was his last chance to win a medal in this grade. He seemed to be everywhere on the field, in the backs, centre-field, in the forwards – wherever the ball was. And when he hadn't the ball himself, he was roaring, rallying, urging on his team mates, inspiring them to give of their best. This was typically Teddy. He was always full of life, bursting with energy and enthusiasm. He couldn't sit still, even in the classroom, where he was always up to some devilment and mischief. But he was at his best on the football field, where all that excess energy could be channelled into chasing the big ball and winning the game. That is why I found it so strange to watch him that day. Because I knew what he himself didn't know yet. His heartbroken mother had told me. He had only six months to live. He was striken with cancer. Sure enough, almost six months to the day, on a cold, wet afternoon in December that same team that carried him shoulder-high off the pitch, were to carry him once more on his last journey to the cemetery.

Of all the things that happen in this life, nothing is more poignant, nothing more tragic, nothing more inexplicable than the death of a young person. Enough to make God himself weep. Twice the Gospels mention that Jesus wept – both were on the occasion of the death of a young person – at the funeral of the widow's son and at the tomb of Lazarus. No words can console the parents for their loss. Nowhere are we more confronted by the mystery of life and the mystery of death.

The first reaction is understandably one of loss, of incomprehension, even of anger. How could God be so cruel? A young life like that with so much promise, snuffed out so wantonly, seems the act of a cruel and capricious god. But time is a great healer and it is always the flowers plucked in early bloom whose fragrance and freshness last the longest. As for all that promise lost, life is strewn with the wreckages of broken promises. Every golden-haired youth doesn't grow into a hero. A promise unfulfilled is often better than a promise broken.

A glance back through the pages of history reveals the extraordinary number of outstanding people who have died in their youth, or at least were plucked in the prime of their life. People like Mozart, the Little Flower, Alexander the Great, Joan of Arc, John Fitzgerald

Kennedy – to name but a few. It would seem the Greeks were right with their proverb, 'Those whom the gods love die young'. Life should not be measured in terms of longevity. Life expectancy is a fiction of modern statistics. Each of us, as Paul said, has his 'appointed time'. When it comes, even if it comes in the early years, it is not a life cut short. It is a life completed. It is no coincidence that Jesus Christ himself died at 33, in the prime of his life or that his last words on the Cross were simply, 'It is completed.'

No fool like an old fool

The first time I noticed her was at a French language course and she stood out like a sore thumb. The age-span of the students there ranged from late teens to the early thirties. She was well on into her seventies. My first impression was that she must be a senile old lady to attempt to learn French at her age. Like most people of my age I thought she would be better employed sitting at home in her armchair, saying her rosary and preparing for the next life. By the time the course was over she may not have learned much French but she certainly taught the rest of us a lesson we won't easily forget. She was a dream student – interested and eager. Her enthusiasm left the rest of us gasping. Every time we were tempted to nod off the sight of this chirpy septuagenarian plying the teacher with her eager questions kept the rest of us on our toes. If there were a competition for 'Student of the Year' she would have won it hands down. I think everybody agreed at the end of the course, that if we were half the person she was at her age, we would be doing alright.

She certainly was a remarkable woman, when you consider what her early school formation was. They were the days when school was a sort of purgatory everybody had to go through before they entered adulthood. Once they got out of school in their late-teens or early twenties, that was it. For better or for worse, they were qualified for life. Even if they were tempted to continue after that, most people had acquired such an aversion for education they would die rather than open a school book. Now the emphasis has changed. Education is far more child-oriented. A great effort is being made to make it a more pleasurable exercise. A lot of tears have been taken out of it. Education is a continuing process that should last as long as life itself. It is the other side of the coin. A child-oriented early education should lead to an education-oriented adult. There is no point in our lives when we can say 'Thus far and no further'; when we can afford to put away our text-books or shut the classroom door for the last time.

It is fashionable to blame most of the trouble in modern life on youth when in fact the opposite offers a more rational explanation. An awful lot can be explained in terms of adults who refuse to grow and to learn in a rapidly changing world. It take two sides to make a generation-gap. Fanaticism, prejudice, bias and bigotry – those ugly sisters that cause so much of the world's conflicts today – are features not of classrooms but of closed minds. What else is a fanatic but a

46

prisoner of a single idea and what else is fanaticism but too few ideas too passionately pursued. What else is prejudice and bigotry but a fear and an insecurity bred out of ignorance. And that ugliest horror of all, religious bigotry – spewing out blood and hate in places as far apart as Belfast and Beirut – what is it but a vicious caricature of true religion.

Unless we make room in our lives for study, for continuous education, unless we accept the principle that learning only ends with death itself, we run the risk of becoming easy prey to rigid dogmatism and vicious prejudice. 'There is no fool like an old fool' as the maxim puts it.

Work

The maker's name

It was a long Summer for Patricia and it is not over yet. In June, she did her examination and went to work in a hotel as a chamber maid the day after she finished. She is still there. The day the results came out was the best day of her life. She got it, by a hair's breadth, 5 Ds. How she got Maths, she'll never know. It was only when the excitement passed after the first week that her real troubles began. She started looking for a job and she is still looking. She thought the world was at her feet. She knows better now. She finecombed the small ads for something suitable. She filled countless application forms, she was even called for a couple of interviews. But she hasn't either the face or the figure that might have compensated for the 5 Ds. And besides, she blew it every time with an attack of nerves. There is a lot more to Patricia than the interviewers see or can be expected to see. She is the eldest of a large family. Her mother hasn't been too well for some time. So she had a lot more on her plate besides her examination. Taking everything into account her 5 Ds were a magnificent achievement. A job now would be a double blessing. It would save her family further expense and she might even be able to supplement the family income.

Patricia, I suppose, is one of hundreds. Employers are not and are not expected to be charitable institutions. Nor indeed would Patricia want their charity. There are always more applicants than jobs and some have to be rejected. Business concerns would scarcely survive if they were receptive to every sob-story that comes their way. But they could have answered her letters, those of them that didn't and they were not a few. She deserved at least that much. At the interview, a little more patience would have been a great help to her. They could have worked harder at putting her at her ease. And even though she had to be let down, she could have been let down a lot more gently. Patricia may not wear a label on her coat. If she did it would read: 'Fragile. Handle with care. There is a real person inside.' And if the interviewer bothered to read the small print, he would make out the Maker's name. It bears the hallmark of quality.

48

Great expectations

It all started when he was very young. All those fabulous toys. He could hardly remember them individually now. In fact, they never made much of an impact on him – something which constantly puzzled his parents. His father seemed to have been far more excited about the electric train then ever he was. But then Oliver was so young, – not much more than four, I suppose, and he didn't see a real train until much later. He had a wrist-watch long before he could read the time. It was, in fact, a pattern all his toys seemed to follow. He got them before he was old enough to appreciate them and by the time he was able to use them the novelty had worn off and he had grown tired of them. And clothes – there was always something new. He never had any of them long enough to become attached. He couldn't even remember his First Communion or his Confirmation suit. It was just another new suit.

As he grew up, Oliver never wanted for anthing. There was a bicycle, football boots, a tennis racquet etc. But then he wasn't any different. Lots of kids in his class had the same things, and were equally unimpressed by them. Indeed, one of his classmates had a miniature set of real golfclubs, but after a few days showing off with them on the local course, he acquired an aversion for golf. He hasn't got over it since.

And so to secondary school. It was about this time he started smoking. It was the thing to do. His pocket money allowance was generous. There was no fuss about extra, for special occasions. His dancing days date from about the same time. He didn't start drinking until a bit later. He can remember well the first time he tried beer. He was about sixteen. He thought the stuff tasted horrible. Mind you, it didn't take him too long to acquire a taste for it.

But don't get the wrong impression. Oliver managed to do his work at school. There were some subjects he really liked, like Geography, and others he worked hard at too because he liked the teacher. There was nothing he enjoyed more than doing one of his own projects. His reports were average. He passed his exam.

That was 18 months ago and he is still looking for a job. At 19, the bottom has fallen out of his life. This is the first time he has ever wanted anything so desperately and he hasn't been able to get it. It is a shattering experience for him. He has lost a lot of confidence in himself in the last 18 months. And no wonder! All his applications have been rejected. He has even applied for things he never dreamed of becoming. He knows there is a recession on at the moment and that there are 250,000 unemployed. All the same, he can't help feeling that in some way he had been conned, conned into believing that he would be handed a job of his choice, – like he was handed everything else all his life – on a plate.

We should be very careful about what we give our children. We won't always be there to play Santa Claus to them. And life, as Oliver has just learned the hard way, may not be so generous.

Dad's golfing partner

'We'll be getting in touch with you.' With a nod of his head and a suggestion of a smile the interviewer dismisses the unsuccessful candidate. But 'hope breathes eternal'. And you leave, believing desperately that you're still in there with a chance, that they *will* get in touch with you. Then the long wait begins. Watching out for the post every day. Rushing for the telephone at the first tinkle. As the weeks pass, slowly your hope dies. You could have been spared a lot of drawn-out frustration had you realised leaving that interview that it was thumbs down for you. You were being let down gently – as they say. In fact you may have been out of the hunt before you ever opened your mouth. Not because you had the wrong requirements for the job – which in many cases are meagre enough – but because you had the wrong pieces of paper to show, the wrong grades in your exams – and dare we admit it – the wrong background and the wrong connections. You can console yourself that there were probably many others who weren't even called for that interview.

'But look, Father, you've got to be realistic about this. In our firm we've got fifty openings and five hundred applicants. Even if we wanted to, we cannot do a screening-in-depth of everyone of them, so we start with the Grade D as the cut-off mark. That brings it down to three hundred. By raising the standard to two honours, we might get it down to 150 or thereabouts. And then we interview those.' The interview, supposedly, sorts out the rest. All sounds very reasonable and above board. But is it? There are certainly a lot of loose ends hanging around. For example, what about the dozen or so applicants without Grade C who figure in the final shake-down? And what about those other considerations? References from important people who never even met the applicant – the result of a carefully contrived casual meeting on the golf course. Dad's bank account, Mother's Bridge Club, the family's long-standing record in the party. I don't think they have to be spelt out for anybody.

Well, what's wrong with doing somebody a favour? One good turn deserves another. But favouritism in job-allocation – unless companies are prepared to create sinecures for their friends – is simply injustice. Every time you do somebody a favour, you are picking somebody else's pocket. Every time you open a door for one of your friend's children, you are shutting it on somebody else's child who had right of admission.

Nobody likes discrimination. We all make disapproving noises about apartheid in South Africa. We are all incensed at the treatment of the Ugandan Asians. But the dirt on our own doorstep very often escapes us. 'That's life,' we say, 'it's a very imperfect world. We don't make the rules, we simply apply them.' If you acquiesce in injustice, you are guilty of it too. Systems of injustice exist at all only because individuals abdicate their responsibility. 'For evil to triumph it is enough that good men do nothing.' Or as Christ put it: 'If anyone declares himself for me in the presence of men, I will declare myself for him in the presence of my Father in heaven.' So stand up and be counted. Every time you declare yourself for some unknown victim of injustice you are declaring yourself for Christ.

Creating jobs

I don't know what Michael himself thinks. I only know what his parents say about him. 'Imagine,' they say, 'he's almost twenty now and still hasn't found his first job. It's nearly eighteen months since he left school. He has tried almost everything – even jobs he wouldn't have considered eighteen months ago. But nothing has come of it. And all this hanging about is not doing him any good either.' They look at me as if I could do something about it or at least say something that might be helpful. But what can I say? That we need 30,000 new jobs every year, that more than half the population is now under the age of 25, that emigration is not on any more, other countries have similar problems. Not very consoling for Michael's parents.

There are other things, too, I could say which would be far less consoling, things I choose not to say. But I can't help thinking them. Both of Michael's parents have jobs – good jobs too. In a country as small as ours with such limited job prospects, two job homes is a luxury we can ill-afford. It is surprising, especially in the small depressed rural towns of this country, the number of homes with two or more incomes coming in. The single-bread-winner seems to be a thing of the past. Jobs always seem to marry jobs nowadays. Teachers marry teachers, and guards marry nurses and so on.

Then of course, there are farmers, whom we always lump together as one more or less depressed sector of the community. But there are farmers and farmers. The small-holder who has to struggle heroically against enormous odds, from natural disasters to rising inflation, and the farmer with the salaried wife, and of course, the new breed of gentleman farmer – two salaries and a nice holding. The sort that can hold on to their cattle when prices are bad and sell them off when the prices go up.

The Irish Bishops in one of their Pastorals stated: 'Men with an already adequate salary or pension, women with comfortable livelihoods and no economic need to work, have surely in present circumstances an obligation not to seek or hold on to jobs at the expense of others, especially younger people who cannot find work.' What else is this but a restatement of the old Christian message: 'Let him who has two coats give to him who has none.' Lest anybody think that this is an oblique attack on married women working, nothing could be further from their minds. Housewives should be paid a salary. After all, we give allowances for children and dole to the unemployed.

What's so radical about paying one of the hardest-working and most vital sector of our society? Only in this way can they have a fair choice between taking a job or making a full time career out of home-making. Surely that suggestion is no more than spelling out what the Bishops mean when they say: 'Society has a responsibility to insure that mothers do not feel economically obliged to work to supplement the family income.'

What has all this got to do with poor Michael? Job creation has to do with all of us. At least we can stop putting all the blame on the Government. There are other culprits nearer home and maybe even in the home. If the government is not the fairy godmother you are looking for, maybe you yourself can play that role, if not for Michael, at least for one of his mates.

Small is beautiful

'Think big', 'expand or die', 'the sky is the limit'. These are the slogans of a world obsessed by growth. Size is what it's all about. From Jumbo Jets and multinational companies to lounge bars and washing powders, big is the operative word. And the message of course – Big is beautiful. With size the determining factor and survival the name of the game, takeovers, mergers, amalgamations are the new trends. Some people might prefer to speak about rationalisation and streamlining. In one of my nightmares, I see an army of bureaucrats descending upon us armed with measuring tapes, giving the thumbs down signal to whatever doesn't measure up to the required size. Then they return to their glass towers in Dublin or Brussels and feed their figures to the almighty computer by whom everything is tagged for development or annihilation. So the sentence of death is passed on all those whose only crime is that they are small – the small farmer, the small shopkeeper, the small school.

I'm not against development, and certainly not against rationalisation. If wiping out the small unit is the price we have to pay for progress, then I accept it. What really worries me is the sort of thinking that goes with it. The tendency to make a virtue out of bigness. The sort of feeling we all have nowadays, that everything is becoming 'bigger and better'. As though 'bigger' always meant 'better'. Whatever happened to old truths like 'Good goods in small parcels'; 'It's the quality, not the quantity that counts'. If that is still true, we have become very reluctant to say so nowadays.

Then, there is the other damaging side-effect of all this cult of giantism. The bigger the organisation becomes, the smaller the individual becomes. Big fish in a small pond become small fish in a big pond. No wonder so many people feel overwhelmed nowadays by a sense of their own insignificance. We seem to meet fewer characters nowadays – small but rugged independent individuals. We are all becoming more and more dependent on Big Brother, be it the State or the company, to solve our problems for us. And we are losing something. A sense of our own uniqueness.

The sort of thing Christ seemed most attached to, the grain of mustard-seed, the yeast in the cake, the lost sheep, the sparrow, the widow's mite. His message was not to 'think big', but to 'think small'.

The image of his Creator

I remember as a child getting a carpenter's set from Santa Claus. I don't think anything in my life has ever given me so much pleasure as this little set of tools. I probably broke more things than I repaired with them but the fascination for craftsmen and their tools stayed with me all through my childhood and adolescence. I think it is a fascination shared by most little boys. I would stand for hours in the blacksmith's forge watching the sparks fly as he hammered the hot iron into shape on his anvil or hang about the carpenter's shop, picking up little blocks of smoothly-planed timber. Nothing quite brings me back to my childhood as much as the smell of newly-sawn timber. But I think my favourite place of all was the shoemaker's. As time went on I was gradually but definitely weaned away from the carpenter's bench and the shoemaker's last and oriented in the direction of books and things intellectual. I am not suggesting that somewhere back there in my childhood a master craftsman was lost but there is some little part of me back there which remained undeveloped.

Where have they all gone in such a short time – all those village shoemakers and tailors, carpenters and blacksmiths? Life, certainly in the country is much poorer for their passing. Nowadays a lot of people are beginning to express alarm at the shortage of skilled labour. Some countries like France have launched a massive campaign to upgrade manual labour. I think we could do with something like that. There is still an awful lot of snobbishness, particularly with regard to jobs.

'Getting on in the world' so often means simply getting a white-collared job. The thing that fascinated me most about Mao Tse Tsung's China was the practice of sending its intellectuals periodically into the rice-fields or the factories to keep them in touch with the working-classes. In this part of the world the popularity of the do-it-yourself hobbies and craft classes, and the practice of physical therapy in medicine seems to suggest man's need for a balanced work-diet.

Christianity itself is deeply rooted in manual labour. Jesus Christ was a carpenter. There were many teachers and philosophers in first century Israel. Yet when Christ chose his first disciples he showed a marked preference for those who worked with their hands. Even that great intellectual Paul was a tent-maker by trade and proud of it. In the early Christian tradition the Benedictine monks placed manual labour in a special position with their motto – *laborare est orare* – to work is to pray. Even the Act of Creation itself in the Bible is depicted as the work of a potter moulding man from clay and moulding him in the image of his Creator. In a world which lays such stress on job satisfaction, maybe we need to remind ourselves that a skilled craftsman often presents a better image of his Creator than a status-conscious but very often disgruntled office worker. When we complain about the wastage of our natural resources, we would do well to consider that vast reservoir of God-given human talents we all neglect so wantonly.

Itchy fingers

It reminds one of a scene in a Wild West movie, where the gang of outlaws ride into town and all the God-fearing people take themselves to their homes and board up the doors and windows until the gang take off again in a flurry of horses' hooves and blazing guns. The scene I have in mind is a much more ordinary everyday occurrence. At four o'clock every day, the schools let loose a swarming mass of teenagers on every sleepy little town in the country and about twenty minutes later a fleet of school buses take off leaving the streets cleared again. Some shopkeepers lock up for that twenty minutes and others sigh with relief as the school buses take off. The reason is pilfering or shoplifting. To suggest that any more than a small handful of students indulge in pilfering would be a gross exaggeration. On the other hand to deny that it is a growing trend would be very naive. Students have freely admitted it to me themselves. Every shopkeeper is aware of the more usual methods employed. Usually they work in pairs. One acts as a decoy, drawing the attention of the shopkeeper while the other makes the snatch.

It is amazing how widespread pilfering has become and in some quarters it has become so acceptable that people even like to boast about their latest acquisitions. After admiring a particularly nice ash-tray once, I was blandly told where and how it was lifted. Many a flat has been fully provided with ash-trays and drinking glasses in this way. There are a lot more people with sticky fingers than we would like to think and this does not include the poor unfortunate klepto-maniacs or those in dire need. It does not seem to be confined to any single section of the community – women seem to concentrate more on smaller items, men go for the more substantial. Building-sites and road-works are happier hunting grounds for them. School cloak-rooms and locker-rooms of all description can have a fatal attraction even for some tiny tots. Unconsciously, most of us have come to accept it as a fact of life. Remember the time and it is not so long ago when it wouldn't occur to you to lock the car. Nobody but a raving lunatic would dream of leaving his car unlocked even for short periods now. A more generally acceptable form of pilfering is finding things. Lost items in the church announcements appear to exceed Found items by at least 10-1. 'Finders keepers, losers weepers' seems to be the guiding principle here. They can't all have disappeared into thin air.

There are almost as many justifications given for it as there are forms of pilfering. Most people like to think of it as some form of occult compensation. It helps to compensate for overcharging. Others like to distinguish between stealing from companies and stealing from people. The same people would be horrified at the thought of picking somebody's pocket. But the greatest justification of all in most people's eyes is the fact most big companies budget for this sort of thing.

It doesn't matter how you try to justify it – the truth is simple. Whether it be worth five pounds or five pence, or the fiftieth fraction of a farthing – it is stealing. The Seventh Commandment states now as it did in the time of Moses, as it always will, 'Thou shalt not steal'. And all the gobbledegook in the world about profit margins, expense accounts, fringe benefits and surplus budgeting won't alter that simple truth.

Missing the bus

They call it 'Monday Morning Blues'. That down-in-the-mouth feeling after the weekend. And, if, as happened today, the week begins on Tuesday, the staff can be very gloomy indeed. Add to this a hangover from celebrating the national holiday in the time-honoured way by 'drowning the shamrock', and I think we might be forgiven if we weren't quite our usual selves this morning. But at best, we showed up. A little ravaged maybe. A bit touchy, perhaps. But, by God, we were there. And that is more than can be said for all the colleagues. Absenteeism is the 21st century sin of omission. Absenteeism was an abuse practised by medieval bishops and 19th century landlords. Today it crosses the whole spectrum from top-executives to schoolchildren. It is no less wrong now than it was then.

Recently I read about a leading car manufacturing company who for the first time in 74 years is going to lose money this year in spite of the fact that demand was never greater. The main reason given for this extraordinary state of affairs is the absenteeism of the workers. It has risen from 9% three years ago to a staggering 17% in the first ten months of last year. The company claims to have lost 10 million hours of work last year. Incidentally, they speak in the trade of 'Monday cars'. I hope you never have the misfortune to buy one.

So much for the car-industry. Anybody familiar with the class-room scene can see that the prospects for the future are not too bright. It is becoming an increasingly rare experience for a teacher to have a full class together for any single lesson. And that, mind you, in spite of the free buses. Ironically enough, one of the more common excuses one hears nowadays is 'I missed the bus, Sir.' God be with the days, and it is only a few years ago, when children cycled miles through rain, hail and snow to school. Attendances were better then. In fact this is one of the most intriguing aspects of the whole question. The more conditions improve, the greater the absenteeism. Absenteeism is probably more prevalent among the younger workers than the older ones. And yet the older ones would in general have taken those jobs because there was nothing else for them, whereas those in their early twenties would presumably have had the benefit of career guidance.

Morally speaking, there are many questionable aspects to absenteeism. What is most distasteful is that when you don't show up, somebody else has to carry your load – you're getting a free ride, on sombody else's back. It is remarkable how often Christ in the Gospels

60

refers to the good and faithful servant. In fact it's the way we are told he will call his chosen ones on the last day. It would hardly seem an appropriate way to greet those whose greatest failing in this life was absenteeism. They run the risk of 'missing the bus' – forever.

The company

Christianity has always suffered from a surfeit of holy people and a shortage of whole people. Integrity lagged far behind in the pecking order of conventional Christian virtues. Piety, conformity, even respectability became the hallmark of the true Christian in a clerically dominated church. Religiosity replaced religion; churchiness replaced Christianity. The Pharisees returned with a vengeance. Happiness, the *raison d'être* of true religion, gave way to the institutional smugness of those who have assured themselves of salvation.

Religion cannot be worn on occasion like a Sunday suit. Life and worship must be integrated into a single whole. The Sermon on the Mount outlines the virtues that make up this wholeness and holiness. They contrast starkly with the attitudes required for worldly success. The poor in spirit are those who are conscious of the illusory nature of human support. 'Put not your trust in princes' breaks the first rule of the old-boy club: 'It's not what you know that counts but who.' Those who mourn do so because they are conscious of evil in the world and sin in themselves. But the man of the world is 'liberated', no scruples or hang-ups. He knows how to bend principles and compromise truth. The gentle, the unassuming, the considerate may well inherit the Kingdom but they won't get very far in the Company. Those who get to the top are pushy and aggressive, whose only interest is self-interest. To win the big prizes you must be hungry and mean. You need a voracious appetite for success. Those who hunger for justice end up on a prison diet like a St Paul or a Sakarov. It is on the backs of the merciful, the pure in heart, the peace makers and the persecuted that the ruthless, the machiavellian, the trouble-makers and the exploiters build their empires.

There are many roads purporting to lead to happiness. Most of them, like power, wealth and pleasure are blind alleys and they are strewn with human wreckage. Our choice is between the ladder of success or the mountain of the Lord, between a coronary or a crown. The beatitudes – 'the happy attitudes' – charter the course which leads to Christ.

Settling old scores

The old cowboy films of my boyhood Sundays had a scene that always intrigued me, indeed shocked my Catholic sentiments somewhat. In the bar-room shoot-out, the gangster, beaten to the draw, tottered to the floor, riddled with bullets. As the gunman turned away, the stricken gangster weakly raised his gun and fired a last shot into the gunman's back. And then he slumped back and died, almost contentedly, a wisp of smoke spiralling from his gun and a flicker of a smile on his face. Sweet revenge.

I accepted all this then as part of the Western fantasy-world. I know better now. Life is full of people with chips on their shoulders, real or imaginary, all waiting for a chance to get their own back. They carry their scars through life, refusing to let them heal until they have settled accounts. Feuds, vendettas and grudges are nurtured in parishes, in streets and even in families. Some are even passed down from one generation to the next. A colossal amount of human energy and ingenuity is expended on settling old scores and exacting vengeance. The *lex talionis* is alive and well and thriving in every human environment, but nowhere better than in the industrial world. Management fingers individuals of their workforce for redundancy. Blacklists are kept. Troublemakers are singled out. The workers too know where and when to call a lightning strike and who in management is to be sacrificed. Even in the corridors of power, in the velvet setting of the plush boardrooms, the knives are long and sharp and are slipped between pin-striped shoulder-blades with a smile.

Honour is always at stake when the God of vengeance is invoked. It is strange that honour is claimed as the motive of revenge. 'Getting one's own back' is raised in our world to the level of a virtue. The injured party could never hold its head up again if the injury is not repaid. Loved ones too are invoked. We owe it to our wives and families. 'Getting even' becomes an obsession. 'I'll fix him if it is the last thing I do.' Shades of the prostrate gangster and his smoking six-shooter! The world has nothing but contempt for the one who turns the other cheek. He is a weakling. He lacks steel. It taunts our weakness. 'He took it lying down.' It goads us on to vengeance. 'Don't let them get away with it.'

What is refreshing about the gospel is that it recognises us as we are, full of pettiness and vengefulness, exacting hurt for hurt, trading blow for blow. No mushy sentimentality about the brotherhood of man and love sweet love. Enemies we all have. The little ones prosecute us, the big ones persecute us. Letting them away with it is not easy. Loving them is a call to perfection.

The hireling

When I go shopping, especially in the bigger stores in the cities, I'm always ill-at-ease. I'm relieved when I'm finished, when I've got what I was looking for. In these big shops I head instinctively for the counter with the older assistant, even though sometimes it is the wrong department. My impression is that from older assistants, men or women, you are more likely to get the human touch. They treat you as a person, they have the experience and the patience to find out what you really need and a genuine wish to satisfy. The 'bright young thing' at the next counter gives the impression of indifference, of wishing to make a sale as quickly as possible. These are impressions, based on very brief encounters and appearances are very deceptive. It may well be that the older are more experienced, more relaxed, more sure of themselves, while the younger, being less sure of themselves, try to cover their inexperience by acting more aggressively, more brusquely. Be that as it may, everyone admits nowadays that service is becoming more and more depersonalised.

While this is true, it is also true that more and more people are engaged in service jobs nowadays, both in the public and the private sector. If you exclude those engaged in manufacturing industries and those working on the land, practically all the rest work in services of one kind or another. Priests, teachers, doctors, nurses, guards, advisers of all sorts and all those engaged in business, the list accounts for an awful lot. If you are looking for evidence of a decline in Christianity, I suggest you take a long hard look at this area of life. Because service of others is Christianity, and the quality of our service is a fair indication of our Christianity. It is not a question of the statutory obligations which our jobs impose on us, the minimum for which we draw our salaries. These are matters of justice and the system usually builds in sanctions to insure that they are carried out.

Efficiency-wise, you could be a very good civil servant, without being either civil to, or the servant of, those whom you are supposed to serve. You could be a very good teacher or doctor, without ever noticing the person who is your pupil or patient. But you cannot be a good Christian and not see Christ in him. As a Christian you cannot wear a sign saying 'office-hours only'. Sickness won't wait on appointments and problems will refuse to be scheduled. Christian service operates best when and where the need is. It should depend only on the size of another's need. Otherwise we are hirelings, hired men, mercenaries. We are paid for what we do and we do only what we are paid for. We are not really serving others, we are serving only ourselves. And when the wolf comes in the form of somebody ravaged by need, frightened by trouble, we run away. 'I'm sorry it's not my department', or 'It's closing time', or 'I'm busy'. Remember that each one you dismiss so unheedingly is Christ and it won't pass unnoticed on Judgement day:

Truly, I say to you, as you did it not to one of the least of these, you did it not to me. (Mt 25:45)

No time

'I'm sorry, I haven't time now.' That little phrase, 'I haven't time' is probably the one we use most often ourselves, and the one we hear most often from others. It is the excuse we give for all our failings, all our shortcomings. We haven't time to call; we haven't time to write, and worse still, we haven't even time to answer letters. Parents admit they haven't got time to take care of their children, and pack them off to boarding-school. I wonder, how many of the ever-increasing broken marriages founder because the couple couldn't give enough time to each other. People used to say about those they didn't like, 'I've no time for so-and-so'. It would appear nowadays, we have no time even for those we love.

And what makes it all so remarkable is that we are living in an age when modern technology has furnished our lives and our homes with all sorts of time-saving gadgets. It is the age of instant coffee and TV dinners, jet-travel and pocket computers. Just go back one generation to your father and mother's time. Remember what it was like to boil a kettle then or to light the fire in the morning. And yet our parents and grandparents very rarely, if ever, complained that they hadn't got time. There always seemed to have been plenty of time for everything then.

Most people think it is all simply a question of better organisation of their time. They envy those highly-organised people who, at least, give the impression of efficiency. You know the type. You are lucky if he gives you five minutes of his time. When you are ushered into his office, he greets you with a glance at his watch and a nod to his secretary, which means if you are still there five minutes later she is to call him. Sure enough, on the dot you are dismissed with another glance at the watch, and you shuffle out apologising for taking up so much of his valuable time. There is the other type who divide up their day into little segments. These are the sort 'you can set your watch by'. They run round all day long with alarm clocks in their heads going off at set intervals to remind them to take their pills or see the dentist or take the dog for a walk. All they ever have to say as they breeze in and breeze out again, is 'I have to run now'. Such people in spite of all their organisation or maybe because of it, have no time.

There is a lot of talk nowadays about the energy crisis. But the great problem facing modern man is not shortage of oil, but shortage of time. Scientists will discover new sources of energy. Only each individual can solve for himself his own time-crisis. And this only by changing his basic attitude to life and living. A time will come for all of us when time will be no more. Only then will we really appreciate why heaven has no time, only eternity. In the meantime, it might help us to reflect on what used to be President Kennedy's favourite quotation from the Bible:

> There is a season for everything, a time for every occupation under heaven:
> A time for giving birth,
> a time for dying. . .
> a time for tears,
> a time for laughter.
> A time for mourning,
> a time for dancing. . .
> A time for keeping,
> a time for throwing away. . . (Eccles 3:1-6)

For he's a jolly good fellow

'And so say all of us.' It is, as they say, a time-honoured custom. And a very nice one. When somebody has spent forty or fifty years at his job, it is only right that his colleagues, should mark the occasion of his retirement in a special way. And indeed the company too. After all, he has literally given the best years of his life to the company. A little presentation, a couple of speeches, a toast, is little enough after a life-time of service. Sure he had his faults. Not always the easiest man in the world to work with. And there are some not all that sorry to see him go. But this is not the time to be small-minded. Nobody grudges him a decent send-off. And everybody dips into their pockets for the couple of quid and the television is bought or the silver tray inscribed. And the compliments fly and the toasts are drunk and even perhaps a few tears are shed. In any case the occasion is fittingly marked.

It is a grand thing alright. That is why it is unpardonable when somebody is overlooked or forgotten. And it does happen. It must be very hurtful. Especially to a man who has himself chipped in for years for everybody else's send-off. And then is let go himself without as much as a thank-you from the company or a good-wish card from his colleagues. That kind of omission is too hurtful not to be calculated. It is always the quiet, unobtrusive conscientious kind who are forgotten.

Of course there are others too forgotten but that is regarded as 'par for the course'. One does not put the charwoman on a par with the managing-director when it comes to retirement. More often than not she won't even get a pension after fifty years of badly-paid service. When she leaves, the occasion is seldom marked. Strange isn't it, how the bigger you are and the better-off you are the bigger the presentation has to be. When the gift is being chosen and the levy being made, the remark is often made, especially when it is the boss who is retiring, that 'a colour T.V. would fill the bill nicely, anything less would be an insult'. And usually he is going out on almost full salary.

It's a very unfair world really. If there wasn't a next world with its rewards and punishments, we would probably have to invent one just to even the score. Another world, where 'the first will be last and the last first', where Christ will greet the charwoman with the words 'Well done, good and faithful servant, because you have been faithful in little things, I will put you in charge of great. Enter into the joy of the Lord.' That is the presentation that really counts, the one where nobody will be forgotten.

Recreation

A treasure

This summer I had a stopover of about 2 hours in J. F. Kennedy International Airport in New York. On an impulse, I rang up an old friend. He dropped everything and came out to the airport for a chat. We were old school friends, very close when we were both in our 'teens. Then he went to America, about twenty years ago. We had both changed a lot in the meantime. But the extraordinary thing was our relationship hadn't seemed to change at all. We took up almost exactly where we had left off twenty years before. We talked freely about our ups and downs, like and dislikes, successes and failures. And then my flight was called and we parted again. I think we both felt better – at least I did – that somewhere in the world, there was somebody to whom I could pour it all out, say it as it is, without feeling afraid of imposing on him or being misunderstood or needing to impress.

That is the extraordinary thing friendship is. We don't always appreciate our friendships the way we should. How easily they get crowded out of our lives. How casually we neglect them. And very often just for the want of a postage-stamp. One hears an awful lot today about love and we all preach charity or have it preached at us. But friendship is a sort of Cinderella among the virtues.

In a world that is becoming daily more impersonal, where even in the bigger cities the great enemy is loneliness, we all need friends more than we realise and all the friends we can make. It is one of the few places left in this world where we can really relax, let it all hang out, be ourselves for a change. People nowadays complain about loss of identity. Perhaps what they are really suffering from is loss of friends. Only with our friends can we really be ourselves. Who else loves us enough to tell us the truth about ourselves? Who else would get away with it? There are a lot of alcoholics who would be cured if they had friends instead of buddies. We would all make fools of ourselves far less often if only we had kept our friends, the sort who wouldn't hesitate to risk even friendship to warn us.

The Bible has many things to say about friends but few finer than the Book of Sirach:

A faithful friend is a sturdy shelter:
he that has found one has found a treasure.
There is nothing so precious as a faithful friend,
and no scales can measure his excellence.
A faithful friend is an elixir of life;
and those who fear the Lord will find him. (Sirach 6:14-16)

The Gospels mention a family in Bethany, where Christ like to visit. Even in the middle of a very tight schedule, he managed to drop in for a visit. In fact it was one of the last places he stayed before his crucifixion. He was so close to them that Martha could give out to him about her sister Mary. If Christ, who was the Son of God, needed the friendship of these two girls and their brother Lazarus, who are we to assume we can survive without friends.

A hundred thousand welcomes

Beautiful new homes have sprung up everywhere. Whole new streets, new estates have been created. Old dilapidated farmhouses have been replaced by modern bungalows. People seem to have become very house-proud. Lawns and gardens are, for the most part, beautifully kept and the houses themselves are tastefully decorated and furnished. Windows are noticeably larger in the new houses as compared with the old. It used to be automatic one time to draw the curtains when the lights were switched on in the evening. Not anymore. At least in the living-room, people tend to leave their curtains undrawn. It is understandably a little bit of show-off. Passerbys are treated to a coy and cosy display of taste and affluence. A sort of 'Ideal Home', complete with Father in his armchair with pipe and newspaper, Mother with her crochet, and the children sprawled on the lush carpet watching television. Another thing I've noticed – and this I find harder to understand – hospitality seems to be on the decline. People don't seem to visit now as much as they used to. And meeting visitors at the door – something unheard-of when I was a boy – seems to be much more common now. Even in clerical circles hospitality is not what it used to be. Older priests decry the lowering of standards in this area in recent times.

Things weren't always like this. I can remember myself in the early fifties being chased out of the sitting-room into the outer darkness, because a visitor had called. He was always given the best chair nearest the fire. The new china was taken out and Mother made up a very enticing tray, God only knows how, at such short notice. And what remained of the whiskey from the previous Christmas was produced. And between Father's insistence and the visitor's protests that 'we shouldn't have gone to all this trouble', he was left in no doubt that he was very welcome indeed. We all kept our fingers crossed that he wouldn't notice the ceiling where the plaster had fallen off or the large hole in the threadbare carpet or the damp stain on the wallpaper. We had our pride then too but not always the means to live up to it. In Grandfather's time, the travelling man was always given a place of honour in the kitchen and a share in whatever meal was going. Ireland was not called 'the land of the hundred-thousand welcomes' for nothing. There must have been a very long tradition behind the 'Céad Míle Fáilte'.

And it is a truly Christian tradition in it's deepest sense. The monasteries were renowned for their hospitality to travellers and strangers. The bible itself was a world where hospitality ranked among the greatest of the virtues. It is actually in terms of hospitality that the Gospel described Christ's rejection: 'He came unto his own and His own received him not.' It is in these very same terms of hospitality that Christ will pronounce His judgement on us on the Last Day; 'For I was hungry and you gave me nothing to eat, I was thirsty and you gave me nothing to drink.'

Make-up

She always sat by the poolside, looking beautiful, while the rest of us splashed about for hours in the water. Needless to say, this was in America and the temperature was somewhere in the low 90's. I often wondered why she didn't jump in and cool off even occasionally. Any woman could have told me. If this divine creature had plunged in – and she must have had great will power not to – it would have taken hours to put all the beautiful pieces back together again. Her hair would be a mess, her make-up would have streaked, her eyelashes would have come unstuck. And her whole day would have been ruined. It seems, that kind of beauty, unfortunately, is not waterproof.

We are living in a very beauty-conscious world. And what makes it unique is that men are almost as beauty-conscious as women nowadays. The men's beauty industry has really mushroomed in the last decade or so. Dad's Xmas present was always the easiest to buy. It was a toss-up between ties, razor blades or tobacco. It must be almost as big a headache as choosing Mother's now.

What harm is there in this beauty consciousness? If looking beautiful makes people feel better and gives pleasure to others as well, it's a good thing, a very good thing; But there are some questionable aspects to it. First of all, it seems to be a very relative thing. Our ideas of beauty change considerably from age to age. The Mona Lisa would not turn many heads nowadays. Even within one's own life-span it changes. Take babies. Everybody thinks they are adorable. Yet they are all small, fat and bald. Whenever some adoring mother asks who baby is like I'm almost tempted to say Winston Churchill. If you are in your thirties or forties and small, fat and bald – and not Winston Churchill – you are no longer adorable. And you better believe it! Our notions of beauty, I think, must be conditioned. Somebody up there is telling us what is beautiful and encouraging us to ape it. That is what advertising is all about.

When we narrow it down to the colour of the eyes, the tilt of the nose or the shape of the mouth, we are debasing the notion of beauty. Because real beauty has to do with the person, not the body. Two beautiful people of recent times, whom everybody recognised as such were Pope John XXIII and Mother Teresa of Calcutta. Neither of them would have measured up to the glossy magazine standards. The most beautiful person whoever lived was Our Lady. She was 'our tainted nature's solitary boast'. She was beautiful precisely because she was sinless. If we spent one-hundredth of the time and energy and expense in being beautiful instead of just looking beautiful, then this world would be a very beautiful place indeed.

Christmas cards

I stopped sending Christmas cards a couple of years ago. I thought it was the right thing to do then. I'm not so sure now. When I was first ordained, I had so many friends. There were all those school-friends who had meant so much to me before our ways had parted. Then, I moved a couple of times, the first few years, from a school to a parish and back to a school again and there were all those friends I picked up along the way. The whole thing was getting out of hand, especially at Christmas-time when it came to sending Christmas cards. No matter how many I sent, there were always the half-dozen New-Year cards, rushed off in haste, to cover those I received unexpectedly from forgotten friends. Then there were the New Year cards I received in return for the Christmas cards I sent to unsuspecting friends. It all became very complicated. And it goes without saying, more and more expensive and indeed more troublesome too. In the end, in a fit of frustration, I cut it out altogether. That year I sent no cards at all. I got a lot that year and I felt quite guilty about it but I resisted all temptations to dash off a few. The following year my Christmas mail was down to a mere trickle and it has remained more or less at that ever since. That was, in its own way a moment of truth for me.

Now that I'm older and I've got my friends down to more manageable proportions I'm beginning to have second-thoughts about sending Christmas cards. I may not be wiser now but I've certainly far less illusions about myself and I'm less inclined to confuse friends with acquaintances. I think, as one grows older one makes less friends or at least, makes friends less easily. But then, on the other hand, we do deepen the few real friendships we've got. I regret now not having sent Christmas cards because I know that among all the acquaintances I have shed, I may have lost one or two real friends. There are a few whose names or faces come to mind at odd times in odd places and I always feel a pang of regret for having neglected them. People move, addresses get lost, new faces crowd old friends out.

The great thing about a Christmas-card is that it keeps people in touch. And while people are in touch, there is always the hope that in more favourable circumstances, old friendships can be revived. I should know. Even in spite of all my neglect, there are still the few old faithfuls who never fail to send me a card. And I'm always touched to think they still remember me after all those years and all that neglect. When you've said everything there's to be said against Christmas cards

– and there is a lot to be said against it – it's a nice custom all the same in a world which is losing a lot of its nice customs. And in spite of the way we abuse it, it is a real Christian one.

Same again, Jack!

Recently, I was watching two little boys playing a game. They were about 4 or 5 years old and they were playing the type of game very young children love to play – pretending to be grown-up. They were perched on two high stools, leaning on their elbows on the side board and pretending to be smoking and drinking. Just as little girls like to play hospital, these two little lads were playing 'PUB.' It was very funny to watch them. They had all the right phrases like – Same again, Jack, Fill 'em up etc. What fascinated me most was one little lad, who every couple of minutes would wipe his mouth with his sleeve, turn to his companion and say 'Be back in a minute.' Then climb down from his stool, toddle outside and return a moment later. I was so intrigued by this that I stopped him on one of his trips and asked him why he kept going out like that. 'What do you do out there?' I asked him. 'Nothin'' he said. 'And why go out then?' ''Cos Daddy always does it' he said. Young kids like that have a remarkable knack of putting their finger on the truth of a thing, very often innocently and unconsciusly.

The in-and-out pattern so typical of most pub-drinking suggests an obsession with quantity, like a beer-drinking competition. There is an earnestness, a seriousness about the drinking, about the actual consumption, that one doesn't notice elsewhere. A certain amount has to be consumed within a limited period of time. There seems to be a pressure there to drink up and get on to the next. I was very struck by the complete difference in drinking habits in a city like Paris. You can spend a whole evening there sitting in a café over a single beer or a glass of wine. And in fact most people do just that. There is no pressure on you to order a second drink. I'm not suggesting that there are no problem drinkers in France or that alcoholism isn't a serious problem there but in the main their drinking pattern seems more civilized than its counterpart elsewhere.

The 'demon drink' is not the culprit we frequently make it out to be. Total abstinence or teetotalism was never intended except for the heroic few. The rest of us are called to moderation. In some quarters even that demands heroism. The old moralists summed it up well with their Latin adage, *virtus in medio stat*. Here, as elsewhere, moderation is not only a virtue, it enhances the quality of life.

RECREATION

Wine is like life to men
  if you drink it in moderation.
What is life to a man who is without wine?
  It has been created to make men glad.
Wine drunk in season and temperately
  is rejoicing of heart and gladness of soul'. (Sirach 31:27-28)

An excellent cause

There were a few of us, committee members, standing inside the door of the dance-hall. It was our job to prevent people gate-crashing the dance. The pubs had just closed and the 'hards' with their pockets bulging with bottles were planning to finish their carousing in the dance-hall and without paying for it into the bargain. There was a festival on in town and the late drinking hours had drawn in the usual unruly element from outside the area. There are always the couple of toughs, well tanked-up, itching for a fight. There I stood in the front line, feeling anything but a hero. I could not help thinking that if I was going to be cut down in the call of duty, a dance-hall brawl is hardly the setting I would have chosen.

It all looks so different now at the time of the year when the festival is being planned. The meetings are enthusiastically attended, the committees are elected and the programme is drawn up. It all promises to be a roaring success. Of course, it is in aid of an excellent cause – re-roofing the church. If anybody has any doubts about the venture, they would not be well received just now.

Festivals play an important part in the life of rural communities. They get people pulling together instead of tearing each other apart. They give people pride in their own localities and they contribute in no small way to the local economy. Above all, they help to relieve the dreary monotony of rural life. Not everybody can afford to take a continental holiday or, for that matter, any kind of holiday. For them the annual festival is the one bright spot in their calendar.

There is no question about it, they are a good idea. If there is any fault to be found with them it is that in practice they don't always measure up to the ideal. The programme always looks far more impressive than the actual events. After the early years they very often deteriorate considerably. 'Chasing the shilling' becomes the main priority. They tend to skimp on the cultural and the athletic events in favour of the more commercial. In some cases, they have degenerated into drinking and dancing festivals. The whole venture becomes little more than an excuse for the 'extension of the drinking hours'. Sometimes, making my way home in the early hours of the morning, I come across some young fellow vomiting his guts out on the side of the road or sprawled out on the footpath in a drunken stupor and I wonder whether I'm doing God's work or the devil's. Even if the church does need a roof badly I wonder is it worth it at that price?

Time, gentlemen, please!

Time, gentlemen, please! and high time we introduced some measure of common-sense into our drinking patterns. Round drinking, i.e. standing a round of drinks for a group is still the normal practice in many places. The man who shirks his round fails the ultimate test of manhood and is shunned like a leper of old. Strange how men often seem to change their personalities in a pub. Tight-fisted men reach for their wallets, trying to beat each other to the draw, like cowboys in an old-style Western. A man not particularly notable for his generosity will throw a tenner on the bar-counter with almost careless abandon when his turn is called and will scoop up the change without so much as giving it a glance.

Basically, it is a pressure, an encroachment on an individual's freedom of choice. Drinking is a very individual thing. What one man needs, another man can't take. Again it tends to speed up the rate of drinking. The man whose turn to stand is next gets his cue from the first empty glass. Fast drinking is more potent than slow drinking. And this is where all common-sense is abandoned. Some are drinking whiskies and brandies; others are drinking beers, stouts and lagers – short drinks and long drinks. Surely these were not meant to be consumed at the same rate. So the amount a man can take, type of drink he takes and rate at which he takes it are all very individual things. If he is joining in a round he is going to have to compromise on these. A man who prefers a half-pint but is standing whiskies is tempted to look for a whiskey back. Above all the man whose limit is two pints is obliged to drink four or more, if he is involved in a round. There are other considerations too. The prices of drinks vary enormously. Peoples' incomes and commitments vary even more. The pound one man spends may be from his surplus while another's may have to be deducted from the family budget. That pound may have been the cause of a row between himself and his wife one hour earlier when she begged for a badly-needed increase in the housekeeping money and he refused. You wouldn't think it, to watch it thrown on the counter now with such cheerful abandon. Round drinking tends to subsidise the better-off drinker while impoverishing the less well off.

And round drinking is exclusive and discriminatory. There is the man whose work brings him into contact with the public when they are in need, like a doctor. The sort of people the public feels indebted to. He may like a drink and a bit of socialising but he has to avoid the local because he knows he will be pestered by too many people, wishing to buy him a drink. And there is the teetotaller, the pioneer. One of the reasons he gave up drink may have been for the good of his family. To have to sacrifice the very pleasant social life of the pub (and in rural Ireland it may well be the only social life there is) is not fair. With round-drinking he cannot afford to socialise.

Why then has round drinking survived? It is a tradition and traditions die hard. It is undoubtedly a very social tradition. And it takes a lot of moral courage on the part of individuals to break traditions and moral courage anywhere is a rare enough thing. People are always asking the moderate majority to assert itself. The response would seem to indicate that majority, if it exists, is largely a spineless one. It is too easy to label the man who buys his own as a 'mean man' or worse still 'no man at all'. Manliness or rather, machoism, is the heart of the problem. As usual, the Bible puts its finger on it:

Do not aim to be valiant over wine,
For wine has destroyed many (Sirach 31:25).

The paid-up member

'Every day,' he said, 'they come in here to my shop, looking for a pair of shoes or a new shirt or maybe an overcoat. If you're lucky they might even offer to pay cash for it. And then they look at the price-tag and you know then your troubles are only beginning. Maybe they won't bother after all. Price-wise, it wasn't what they had in mind at all. And then the bargaining begins. They'll haggle over every last penny. Finally, when they've got the discount and more or less satisfied themselves that you're an extortionist and racketeer, they leave with their purchase. And you will meet the exact same people in the pub that night standing a round for their friends. And when it comes to paying for it, they'll take a fistful of money out of their pockets and say to the barman "Here! Take what you want out of that," and they won't even bother to count their change.' I heard that story recently from an obviously disgruntled shopkeeper. While I do accept it is very much one man's point of view – I do think there is a moral in it somewhere.

There always seems to be a shortage of money for essentials but no great scarcity for luxury items. Strange isn't it, that it is nearly always essentials that we get on credit while we almost always pay cash for our luxuries. And if we are in debt – who isn't these days – it is almost always for essentials like our house and car, our clothes and groceries. We don't owe the publican anything or our golf-club or the bingo. In fact there is a strange kind of honour attached to paying our club subscription and our round of drinks which doesn't hold good at all with regard to our grocery or drapery bills. The most we can lose here is loss of credit which can be offset by taking our custom eleswhere. But in the golf-club our honour is at stake.

Of course, it's hard to blame people. We were all brought up to accept the new commandment – 'Buy now, pay later'. The never-never system is beautiful as long as there is no day-of-reckoning. But there are small businesses everywhere struggling, some of them desperately, in the present economic climate, to survive. What is putting them to the wall is the huge load of bad debts they are carrying. They can't pay their way because we couldn't pay ours. Before we decide to give up cigarettes or drink for Lent we might take a close look at our accounts and find out what is outstanding there. We might even find we haven't really been paying for our drinks at all, all these years. Our draper or our grocer or our banker has. While we owe them, giving up things for Lent is only an exercise in self-delusion. Living within our means which is giving up what we cannot afford, is probably the greatest form of self-denial most of us could practise.

No strangers

'Name?' she said without lifting her eyes from the form on the desk. I gave her my name. She wrote it down. 'Date of Birth?' and still she didn't look up. And so it went on until the last line had been completed, and all I could see of her was the top of her head. I still had hopes of some slight acknowledgement of my existence. 'Next please!' she said, putting away my form and taking out a new one. As I left, a feeling of deadness came over me.

Professionalism is becoming more and more a feature of modern life. It makes for greater efficiency. And better service too. It's all part of a new life-style, resulting from urbanisation. The last hundred years or so has seen a massive change in social living. Nowhere is this change more starkly evident than in the deserted villages and teeming cities. The intimacy of the small town or village is giving way to the anonymity of the city. How people relate to each other is deeply affected. Old virtues need new techniques. Of these, courtesy seems the virtue most threatened.

In its rural setting courtesy comes easy. It depends heavily on the closeness of relationships there. Everybody knows everybody else and all about them. Each person is an individual, a character in his own right. People are not referred to by the jobs they do but as individuals. Nobody speaks of the milkman, the postman, the grocer. It is Mick or Tom or Joe. The pace of small-town life allows plenty of time to meet the demands of courtesy. The village housewife looks upon shopping not as a chore but as an opportunity to do a bit of socialising. Visitors remark on the old-world charm of this style of life. They don't always realise that village sociability can often mask murderous hate, ignorance and intolerance. Also failure in courtesy carries bigger penalties in smaller communities. Above all courtesy depends on intimacy. People greet each other and smile at each other because they know each other.

Christ said: 'If you greet only those who greet you, are you doing anything exceptional? Even the pagans do as much.' Christian courtesy demands more. And nowhere is this demand made more than in the cities and other densely-populated areas of modern life. In the course of a single day one meets hundreds, maybe thousands of people and all of them unknown. If they are known at all, it is by the functions they perform. They are shop assistants, bus conductors, garage attendants. They are categories, not individuals. Motorists, pedestrians, clients, customers etc. Relationships are professional rather than personal. Precisely because it is impossible to relate to them as individuals it is possible not to treat them as persons. People do complain of being treated as 'just another number', of becoming depersonalised in the bigger centres.

As the change from rural to urban is relatively new, most people's attitudes are still those of the small town. Since small-town courtesy doesn't work in the city, there's a real danger that courtesy itself may be down-graded. What is required is a new technique, a new attitude of mind. The 'don't-talk-to-strangers' mentality must go. Like the child who 'makes strange' with people, the cause of the trouble is in the mind. In a very real sense there are no strangers except those created in the mind. The shyness-of-the-stranger complex should be left behind in the country. One simple way of dispelling strangers is by smiling. It would be a pity if the smile were to become the preserve of the business world where its value is shrewdly assessed and fully exploited. It would help too to look people in the eyes when talking to them. The eyes can often show the concern for others that words don't always express. And courtesy, is above all showing concern for others.

The adventures of a fiver

In the old days there was an essay in the school reader called 'The Adventures of a Shilling'. A shilling was a day's wages then. The Adventures of a Fiver, − to take its modern equivalent − would make a great short-story or perhaps a T.V. play now. Or indeed, a whole series, for that matter. It would be fascinating to follow its journey from person to person, pocket to pocket, hand to hand. From the crisp new note, fresh off the printing press to the battered old bill consigned to the furnace in the bank vault. Oddly enough, in a world so obsessed by hygiene, nobody ever dreams of washing their hands after handling it and certainly, nobody is ever detered from taking it even from the most suspect sources. How many would refuse it, even if they were absolutely sure it came from a highly contagious leper?

Strange isn't it, how we never think of its past. Yet every crease in it, every stain on it, has its own story. It must have brought a lot of happiness to many people. There is no doubt too, it must have left a long trail of misfortune behind it. It might have bought the medicine that cured the sick child or the fuel that brought warmth into the life of an old woman, or food for a deserted mother and her children. Think of all the presents it might have paid for, toys for children, birthday presents, the tokens of love from a boy to a girl, husband to a wife or a child to its mother. Think of the new coats, the new hats, the new shoes, the new dresses and the new books. And the pleasure they gave. These are the joyful mysteries of the fiver.

Think, then, of the other side, the seamier side, the sorrowful mysteries. It is not called 'the root of all evil' for nothing. The drink it paid for that started the alcoholic. It might have bought drugs for a teenager. It might even have paid for the body of a prostitute, if it comes that cheap. But it is certainly somebody's price and doubtlessly, somebody has been bought with it. Perhaps to look the other way or keep his mouth shut or fiddle the books. Despite its innocent appearance, it has figured in a lot of sordid deals, bribes, blackmail, kickbacks, backhands. Or phrased more acceptably, for services rendered and favours done. There is a good chance too, that it is bloodstained. Unfortunately, there is a red pound as well as a green pound. It may have paid for the bullet that killed the young mother caught in the crossfire, or the terrorist's bomb that maimed the young waitress for life. And the child who wakes up every night screaming because it cannot forget the sight of Daddy, shot dead as he answered the door. That fiver paid for a child's insanity as well as a man's life.

But it has one great virtue. It does not carry forward its past. It is a crisp new fiver in every eager new hand. In these days of devaluation and inflation and shrinking purchasing power, it is worth reminding ourselves when we look despairingly at the fiver in our wallet, that the only devaluation that matters is the use we make of it. If we insist on spending it, as so often we do, on drinking and shoddy entertainment and shallow status symbols, we should not be so surprised at how little it can buy. It can still buy an awful lot for somebody in real need. In a world where millions die of disease and starvation, you can still get a lot of real value for money. A fiver well-spent can never be devalued.

The big catch

Fish are funny creatures. They're always so busy and yet so pointlessly busy. Ever on the move, they flit about, dashing and darting hither and thither, full of agitation and enthusiasm. How easily they are alarmed by every ripple, every shadow on the water! Always keyed-up, on the alert, so ready for the unexpected, and yet so easily duped, so quick to react to the first rumours of danger and yet so easily caught.

And what about us, the fish Christ sent Peter out to catch? Are we so different? Here we are, immersed in a sea of troubles and distractions, alarmed and agitated by every ripple of excitement, every shadow of doubt that crosses our paths. We expend so much energy on trivialities. We dally so dangerously with temptations, and allow ourselves to be hooked to so many creature comforts from cigarettes to status symbols. It is astonishing that we survive at all.

The miracle of Genesareth is the miracle of our lives. Peter has thrown out his net over us, a net of grace. Like the fisherman's, it moves unseen beneath the surface. And we are drawn into it, in spite of the storms and the currents and the baits with their cunningly concealed hooks. And in spite of our own struggling.

Peter knew the lake well, every pool and every feeding spot in it. And he knew the fish. 'We have laboured all night and caught nothing' was more than a confession of failure. It was a humble recognition of his own inadequacy against the power of nature. We may be keen judges of the world and its ways. We might well be accurate in our judgment of individuals. But we cannot but have a miser's notion of the sufficiency of God's grace. There is no telling what the catch will be like until the net is drawn in on the last day. Like this miraculous draught, it might well astonish even the seasoned fisherman. Who knows what queer fish will be caught there, spluttering and gasping at the size of God's mercy? The 'big catch' is Christ's answer to those prophets of gloom who would put so many out of the reach of God's mercy.

Attitudes

Keeping your head down

The American golfer Lee Trevino once said: 'There are two things you gotta keep your head down for – golf and praying.' It's the golden rule of golf. But it seems to be gone out of fashion in religion at the moment.

We can all remember the days not so long ago when private prayer was a big thing in our lives – morning and night prayers, rosaries, novenas, visits, vigils, adorations, aspirations, etc. We remember too the criticisms that were levelled at this form of religion. There was too much lip-service and time-punching. Above all, religion had become solely a matter of church-going and became divorced from real life. People taunted us with being Catholics rather than Christians.

Then in the last decade or so the emphasis changed. The pendulum swung. And as is the way with the pendulum, it kept on swinging, right through the centre to the other extreme. And that is roughly where it stands today. Mary has become Martha. 'We are anxious and upset about many things' – the plight of itinerants, proper housing for slumdwellers, food for the famine victims of Ethiopia and Sudan. It's the 'Ask not what God can do for you but what you can do for God' age. It's action not adoration, protest not prayer. We've got up off our knees and started marching, 'We shall overcome' is our proud new hymn.

We have forgotten Christ's warning. 'Without me you can do nothing.' We have failed to grasp the simple truth that if all prayer and no action was bad then all action and no prayer is equally bad. We like to believe that Christ spent his life 'going about doing good'. And that the kind of good he did took an awful lot of going about. But with all his going about, he was never too busy or too tired to pray. And the sort of praying he did required getting away from it all. He went up the mountain alone, and out into the desert and across to the other side of the lake. Even in the quietness and darkness of the Garden of Gethsemane, the night before he died, he had to get away from his closest friends, to pray. Surely, if Christ the Son of God, in a far quieter and far more leisured time than ours had to get away from it all to pray, it is an arrogance on our part to assume that we can manage without private prayer.

One thing is certain about prayer – the less you do, the harder it becomes. The reason why we find it so difficult now may not be because it is out of tune with the times we live in but simply that we've lost the knack of it. And to get the knack of it again two things are essential – a time and a place for it. 'I don't have to go to church to pray' people tell you. If you can do it elsewhere then more power to you! If you have the sort of job that provides those quiet intervals when you can switch off from problems and turn on to God – then you're very lucky and don't let your employer know about them. If you have the sort of home where there's not always something to be done, where the T.V. and radio can be switched off without causing a major incident, where the children are seen but not heard, where the wife knits quietly without a tongue in her head – then you've no problem with prayer, though you may have other problems. Otherwise you've got to arrange for it. Prayer doesn't just happen. As Lee Trevino says 'You've got to keep your head down.' You've got to climb a mountain or find a desert. God can't be expected to shoulder his way into your life. It's a poor life that hasn't got a few moments of peace and quiet in it, on a regular basis. All the best doctors recommend it. And it's a poor world that hasn't got some corner in it for prayer. It's what gives life its direction and problems their perspective. To paraphrase the poet:

A poor world this if full of care
We have no time for any prayer.

Blind man's buff

'I see,' said the blind man, who didn't see at all. As a little boy, I thought that terribly funny. Blindness, for children, seems to hold no horror at all. They love even to fake blindness in many of their games like Blind Man's Buff. Maybe it is because they are so terribly afraid of the dark that they always make a game out of blindness. If only blindness could always remain a game children play.

But it is not so and of all the forms blindness takes among adults, physical blindness is probably the most uncommon and the least terrible. Just look at the North of Ireland – the bombing, the maiming, and the killing. You don't have to look any further to see people who are blinded by hate and ignorance, fear and prejudice. The terrorist who sees only the sacredness of his own cause and nothing else. Certainly not the little child whose father he has come to assassinate. He certainly doesn't see his brother in other men or Christ in all men. There is hardly a country in the world that doesn't suffer more or less from the plague of terrorism. 'I see,' says the terrorist who doesn't see at all.

There are those in high places and in places not so high, who cast a blind eye on all the corruption, fiddling and dishonesty that surrounds them. The Watergate cover-up, the Lockheed scandal are probably only the tip of the ice-berg. The kick-back, the back-hand, the fiddled books, the doctored accounts are by no means confined to gangster-movies. How many of that vast mountain of presents which changes hands especially at Christmas time, are – dare we say it – little pay-offs in their own way? 'I see', says the businessman who doesn't see at all.

Then there are the more unfortunate forms of blindness. Those pitiable creatures who've got their lives locked up in blind alleys, from which they can see no way out. People like the unfortunate alcoholic. The sad thing about the alcoholic is that, blind drunk or cold sober, he cannot see what is only too painfully obvious to his wife and children and everybody else. That he is an alcoholic. Because he doesn't see that, he cannot even take the first step out of his own private hell. 'I see,' says the drinker who doesn't see at all.

As for the rest of us, who pride ourselves on our sharp eye, our balanced view, our long-term perspective, how blind we are to our own shortcomings, how often we close our eyes to the crying needs even in our own immediate circle, not to mention the poor, the old, the handicapped? How often we try to take the speck out of our neighbour's eye while neglecting the beam in our own. 'I see,' says the neighbour who doesn't see at all. And so we go on, blindfolding ourselves with one -ism or another. Such is the Blind Man's Buff we grown-ups play. And the sad thing is that, unlike children, we think we can see.

It was remarkable that in all the world when Christ was born, only three unknown strangers, – whom we rightly call the three Wise Men – could say, 'We have seen his star in the East and have come to adore him.' And of all those who followed Christ, looking for this, that and the other thing, there was only one, a blind beggar called Tim in the city of Jericho, who asked simply: 'Lord, that I may see.' Like Tim we are all blind beggars and his is a little prayer we could all say and often.

In God We Trust

It all seems so long ago, now. Almost as though it were a different age in history. And yet, except for those in their teens and younger, we all went through a very similar childhood. For me it was the late forties and early fifties. Some of you probably remember the last war or the depression during the thirties, or even the First World War. They were hard times. And poverty breeds its own virtues. The great virtue of my own childhood was 'waste not, want not'. Nothing was ever thrown away. Garbage disposal was no problem then. Most things disintegrated long before they got that far. Remember the woollen socks darned out of recognition. When they could no longer be used as socks, they started a new life as dusters or mops. Remember the cardboard cut-outs for the leaking shoes. If you came in the middle of a large family, most of your clothes were probably hand-me-downs. Life then seemed to be one big salvage operation. I can still remember the tin box on the mantlepiece where all sorts of bits and pieces were stored, like buttons and safety-pins and pieces of string. And there was always a use for them.

I learned my lesson well then – so well in fact that I now find myself in a completely different world facing middle-age with one obsolete virtue. My problems now is not how to salvage things but to dispose of them. I've got what the Americans call a hang-up. Some people are secret drinkers. I'm beginning to think I'm a secret hoarder. At least I'm very reluctant to part with things. I'm always promising myself that one of these fine days, I'm going to have a real big bonfire. But I never do. I've never got over the old tin-box on the mantlepiece. I've got what might be called a nest-egg obsession.

In the old days there was much more trust in God's providence. 'God will provide' we used to say. And He did. At least we all survived. Nowadays with greater affluence, and smaller families and a welfare state that guarantees to look after us from the cradle to the grave, we've gained much more security alright. But we've lost something too. Trust in God's providence. Ironic though it is, the American dollar carries the inscription 'In God we trust'. The God we trust now is the almighty dollar.

The price of a pearl

There is no greater indictment of the quality of life than the sight of an old man hanging on desperately to his holding. To him, this miserable patch of grass and bog is his only insurance against abandonment and frustration. But hanging on is not the answer. It only sows bitterness and frustration in sons whose best years are squandered in waiting. Sons who themselves never learn from the mistakes of their fathers. Love alone can guarantee security and care in one's declining years. Possessions provide only the illusion of security.

Elderly farmers are not the only people who hold on to things for security. Others have their own holdings from which only death can separate them. It may be property and wealth or status and prestige or power and influence. It may even be an awful lot less – trivial comforts and an easy life. It may not be an easy life at all. It may be a sixteen-hour day or the thankless responsibility of high office. Or a reputation we can no longer live up to. There is nothing more pathetic than an ageing beauty queen who refuses to accept the ravages of time.

Possessions come in many forms. It is not so much these possessions that we must rid ourselves of as the demon of possession itself that must be exorcised. Poverty has become a dirty word in the world we live in. We should not let an Ethiopian famine or a Bangladesh disaster make us forget that poverty is also a Christian virtue. And a very vital virtue for us who live in the rich man's club and eat at the rich man's table. It is no accident that Christ began his Sermon on the Mount with 'Blessed are the poor in spirit for theirs is the kingdom of heaven' (Mt 5:3). Or that the only condition laid down for his followers was that 'they leave all things'. Or that the rich young man should have failed all because he failed this one test, 'for he had great possessions' (Mt 19:22). Or that the pearl in the parable could only be bought by 'selling everything he owns' (Mt 13:44).

The trouble with most people is that they want it both ways. All this and the good life too. But they can't have it both ways. There is a pearl for every man. And there is a price for every man to pay. A price tailored to his own individual circumstances. Detachment is the price. To be able to walk away from what we want most without so much as looking back with regret. Our tragedy is not that we cannot find the pearl but that we are unwilling to pay the price.

Moment of truth

It happened like this. I was taking a walk down the street. As a priest, I was greeted and saluted by all and sundry. People tried to catch my eye as I passed. Little old ladies smiled through windows at me. Men in doorways lifted their caps or touched their forelocks. And then it happened – out of nowhere, a tramp confronted me. It was too late to alter course and I knew it. And half the street had ringside seats. The tramp had arranged it superbly. Years of practice, I suppose. He spun some yarn about his mother in hospital and needing the busfare to visit her. I don't remember really what he said. The truth is, I wasn't listening. I'd heard it all before so often and there was a strong smell of drink off him. It wasn't his first time telling this story either. He related it with about as much feeling as a child giving out a poem in class. Besides, I was busy fingering the loose change in my pocket to insure that, when I drew, it wouldn't be fifty pence I had in my hand. I was beaten, and all I could hope for now, was to cut my losses. We were probably both relieved when the money changed hands, and the incident was over. He shuffled his way up the street – the people disappearing as he approached. While I resumed my walk, down the street, greeted, saluted, smiled at, as before.

Which of us went our way more justified in the sight of God? Or to put it bluntly, which if us was the bigger tramp? There was I, another Christ in the eyes of the people and respected by them as such. And I carried off my part well. Giving alms to the poor as was expected from one of Christ's ministers. Even if it was only ten pence. I had fulfilled God's law and I had edified the people. Not bad for ten pence.

There are times in our lives when the scales fall from our eyes and we see ourselves as God sees us, as we really are. And this encounter is one of these times. It's a rare grace to get – a God's eye view of oneself. As God saw it, we were two brothers – one a lost sheep, looking for help; the other masquerading as a shepherd, but in fact, a hireling. Instead of helping the tramp I got rid of him – with ten pence. The tramp may have thought he 'conned' me out of ten pence, but the truth is I conned him with ten pence. Because I got the better side of the bargain. He cured me, at least momentarily, of my hypocrisy whereas I left him where I found him, in despair. On an occasion like this, some might be inclined to look at the tramp and think 'There but for the grace of God go I'. But the thought that vexes me is – 'There goes the grace of God and I've been found wanting.'

Fear not

It is like a plague that nobody can escape. Everybody suffers from it. It mars the development of children, it torments the adolescent. It affects newly-weds. It ravages those in their forties and it haunts the old. Adolescence and the forties are generally regarded as the crisis years. It comes in a wide variety of forms. Nervousness, stress, tension, pressure, anxiety. It manifests itself in countless ways from a nervous tic to a nervous breakdown. Easily enough diagnosed, seldom if ever, cured. In plain, honest-to-goodness English, it is what we call fear.

We're afraid of something all of the time and of everything some of the time. We're afraid of failure. We're afraid of letting others down and of being let down by others. We're afraid to love somebody because we're afraid they won't love us. We're afraid of losing our jobs, our health, our security, our grip. We're afraid of growing old and of dying. Most of all, we're afraid of being afraid. There seems to be no way out. Like the old Negro in the song 'we're tired of living and scared of dying.'

More and more people are unwilling or unable to cope with their fears alone. Anxiety and worry is undermining their health. For many nowadays, it is becoming impossible to get through the day without taking a pill. For some, getting through the night is even worse. 'Got a problem – take a pill' seems to be the new creed. Every bedside table has its phial of tablets. Every bathroom closet is full of them. Painkillers, tranquillisers, stimulants, sedatives and sleeping-tablets. And while our consumption of pills is increasing all the time, our fears are in no way diminishing.

I sometimes wonder whether there is some connection between the fall-off in prayer and our increasing dependency on pills. People used to talk one time about 'the consolations of religion', how their faith was a great help to them in times of stress, how they could accept any misfortune as God's will. Remember the old days. The old woman sitting by the fire fingering her beads. All gone now, like the thatched cottages. Her modern counter-part is more likely to be heavily sedated watching T.V.

Christ had this to say to the worried and the anxious:

> Therefore do not be anxious, saying, 'What shall we eat?' or 'What shall we drink?' or 'What shall we wear?' For the Gentiles seek all these things; and your heavenly Father knows that you need them all. But seek first his Kingdom and his righteousness, and all these things shall be yours as well (Mt 6:31).

The sign of the cross

She suffers from insomnia – or so she says. She takes a sleeping pill every other night. In fact she is a great believer in pills, particularly tranquillisers. She always resorts to one whenever she is upset, just to get her through those regular domestic crises. She is a housewife, in her mid-thirties, with two young children. Her husband has a good secure job with promising promotional prospects. They live in a well-equipped, semi-detached house in suburbia. A million light-years away from the farm where she was born. And from her mother who raised nine of them without electricity or running water and ran the little farm as well while her husband worked seasonally in England. Her mother, no stranger to trouble, was a placid, jolly sort of woman who took everything in her stride. She wasn't troubled by insomnia. She fell asleep instantly every night from sheer exhaustion. In this as in many other respects, mother and daughter were worlds apart.

Inevitably, with the raising of the standards of living we've all become different from our parent's generation. Certainly, we've all become softer. Compared to them, we've all a very low tolerance of any form of pain or discomfort. We bombard the doctor with all sorts of trivial complaints. We have pills for all sorts of ills, real or imaginary. We want to take the pain out of living. We yearn for a trouble-free existence. A sort of Utopia, where we can have success without effort, French without tears, roses without thorns. In matters of conscience, we've been chipping away for some time now at anything that smacks of punishment either here or in the hereafter. There is an old moral principle which states: 'Nobody is bound to the impossible'. It seems nowadays to have been watered down to 'Nobody is bound to the uncomfortable'. Self-denial, abstinence, sacrifice are dismissed as weird practices from an ignorant and superstitious past.

We've come a long way from the world our parents lived in. But they probably had a vision of life far closer to reality than we have. And certainly far closer to Christianity. Suffering for them was part and parcel of living. The great myth of modern life is that perfect happiness is attainable. As Ivan Illich put it in a talk to doctors: 'Perfect health is held before us as the absence of discomfort whereas in reality it is the ability to cope with discomfort.' And sadly, it is this ability we are losing by our dependance on drugs and alcohol. Maybe the older people were too fatalistic, too pessimistic, too prone to accept misfortune as the will of God. But at least they knew that you can't take the cross out of Christianity any more than you can take the pain out of living. And that crosses are burdens you carry on your shoulders not just pretty ornaments you wear round your neck.

Mere Children

'Put your hand in the hand of the man from Galilee' was the refrain of a fairly recent pop-tune. Putting a hand in somebody else's is the characteristic gesture of a child. Only to parents will a child give its hand unquestioningly. It implies complete trust. No amount of cajoling will entice it to take the hand of a stranger. Once outside the familiarity of the home, a child confronted with a big and frightening world becomes acutely aware of its own smallness and helplessness. Without father's hand, it wouldn't dare venture out. Holding his hand there is nowhere it will not venture. The child is not only willing to be led, it positively wants to be led. The sad thing about growing up is that we lose our fathers or abandon them. In any event we outgrow our need of them. And having lost the need for parents, God becomes very remote for us. Only children instinctively understand God-language. Every child's father is God to him. And God to every child is his Father. Thus is God 'revealed to mere children'.

Growing up means becoming more independent. Or rather ceasing to be dependent. We exchange a child's dependence on people for an adult's dependence on things, like money, alcohol or drugs. And things are notoriously fickle. The world of an adult is a stress-ridden, anxiety-plagued place. Living becomes a matter of coping. Survival is the name of the game. Grey-hairs, ulcers, blood-pressure are the scars of this fight for survival. There is no escaping the tension. Drugs provide temporary relief but never reach the underlying causes. Because these are spiritual. Contentment is a quality of the soul. A state of harmony between a creature and his creator, a child and his father. Adam and Eve unfortunately grew up. They lost their innocence. The original sin was Adam's pride, his ambition 'to go it alone'. It has tainted our nature ever since.

It has left us all 'labouring and over-burdened'. Labouring under illusions of grandeur and burdened with conceit. The heaviest load we have to carry is the load of our own unfulfilled ambitions, the burden of our ego. We've grown too big for our boots. Only humility can restore our lost innocence and our lost paradise. The humility to accept our creature-status, our child-status. To recognise our Father in God, we need to be led. We must learn to want to be led. We must trade childish pride for child-like humility. We must 'put our hand in the hand of the man from Galilee', if we hope ever to find our way home.

Nothing sacred

Recently, after distributing Holy Communion to a fairly large congregation, I inadvertently dropped one of the Sacred Hosts. It can happen to the most careful of priests. When I was back at the altar, one of the servers touched me on the arm. 'Here,' he said, 'you dropped this', handing me a host. It could have been my handkerchief. I don't want to be unfair to the boy, but I was surprised by his casualness. I remember, on another occasion, while carrying the Monstrance during a Corpus Christi procession, seeing two young people on the pavement. A lad and his girl friend. He had a cigarette struck in his mouth and his arm round the girl. They both stared insolently at us, as we passed. We could have been a circus. I felt pity rather than anger for them. A sort of 'Father forgive them for they know not what they do'. There was something missing in them. A sense of the sacred.

They are children of their time. Their attitudes are a fair reflection of the community they belong to. It is all part of the price we pay for change – particularly in religion. Nobody would dream of advocating a return to the extreme reverence of pre-Vatican II Catholicism. Remember what it was like then. Especially the scruples – fretting over the crumbs swallowed before receiving or worrying over touching the Sacred Host with one's teeth. And priests suffered even more. Remember the ones who used to repeat each of the Latin words of Consecration to eliminate all possibility of the Mass being invalid. Many a good priest suffered agony with scruples. And confession was a big bogey. Some people were more obsessed with fear of committing sin in confession than with the relief of having their sins forgiven. Small wonder that confession is now the area where the reaction has been greatest. Looking back on those days, we can now see that the vast energies spent on scruples might have been better spent. Change, when it did come, came none too soon.

We run the risk of losing our feeling of reverence for things religious, our sense of mystery in the presence of the divine, our sense of the sacred. Some loss of reverence is inevitable – with the Mass in English, and lay-readers in the sanctuary, the guitars and the folk-hymns. And a good deal of what is lost is 'piotiousness' rather than piety, sanctimoniousness rather than sanctity. Even so, there's a great tendency nowaday to reduce God to our level, to rub shoulders with Him. We're uncomfortable on our knees, we're unaccustomed to looking up to people. We dislike standing on ceremony even in God's presence. Informality has its own charm. It also has its own place. And worship is not the place for it. Hence the special language and gestures and clothes used there. They help to lift it out of the ordinary because it is not the ordinary. They help to express however poorly, the sacredness we should feel in the presence of God. One thing is sure, if God isn't sacred for us then there's nothing sacred in our lives any more.

False prophets

'Beware of false prophets' (Mt 7:15). There is an old-fashioned ring about it. It sends the imagination leaping back to those faraway ages where wild and bearded old men thundered out dreadful warnings from an angry god to a stiff-necked people. Nothing could seem more remote from a twentieth-century congregation. Surely Christ only meant the warning for His own audience? Or possibly He was speaking metaphorically? If so, we could use it now to let off steam about all those -isms and ideas so comfortably remote from ourselves and our congregations.

All that presupposes, of course, that we buried the last of the real prophets with John the Baptist. Unfortunately, most of us believe that. We don't seem to realise that we ourselves are prophets, real prophets, and in fact the least of us is greater than John the Baptist (Mt 11:11). When the bishop made the sign of the cross with chrism on our foreheads at Confirmation he made us prophets or official witnesses of Jesus Christ in the world. He put that sign on our foreheads to remind us not to be ashamed of it. We should hold up our heads and let the world see that we believe Jesus is the Son of God and we are His prophets. And this is a sobering thought. Others have a right to judge Christ on our showing of Him.

And that is where we can play Him false. The president of the Saint Vincent de Paul Society can underpay his employees. The daily communicant can carry vicious gossip home from church. In a thousand other little things, where God has need of us to carry His grace to others, we can fail Him. These are the times when we are too busy blowing our own trumpets and waving our own banners to notice that God needs us for a moment. Worse still, we can on occasion 'use' Christ for our own purposes. Religion can be a political and social asset. But these are the short-term aims of short-sighted men. And their success is short-lived.

Of the final reckoning, Christ has said: 'Not every one who says to me "Lord, Lord" shall enter the kingdom of heaven.' The last scene in the career of a false prophet is tragic but inevitable. His last appeal, 'Lord, Lord', serves only as a reminder to God of his life of lip-service. He has left God no alternative but to sum up his past and settle his future with a mere four words: 'I never knew you' (Mt 7:23).

Sign of peace

One of the most palpable signs of reform since Vatican II has been the liturgical changes. The priest faces the people, the altar is brought closer to them, English has replaced Latin. The lay people read the lessons. Tucked away beneath the host of other liturgical changes is the Sign of Peace. It is sometimes, particularly in this country, dismissed as just another tiresome rubric. It has been very slow to win widespread acceptance among the people. There are still some who choose that moment in the Mass to rummage in a purse for a handkerchief or bury their nose in a missal. The effusive middle-aged female who threatens to throw her arms around all and sundry, is not contributing to its acceptance. And it is a pity. Because of all the myriad liturgical changes since Vatican II, the Sign of Peace is the most radical, the most biblical and the most needed.

It traces its origins all the way back to the Sermon on the Mount. 'Go first and be reconciled with your brother.' Unless we put reconciliation among ourselves as the basis of our worship of God, our religion goes no deeper than that of the scribes and Pharisees. Our Sunday liturgy, in spite of its colour and charm and community cosiness, is a hollow ceremony unless the Sign of Peace represents a genuine effort for harmony and reconciliation. It is no coincidence that this symbolic gesture is placed immediately before Communion. The message is loud and clear. If you cannot reach out the hand of friendship to your neighbour, you cannot put it out to receive God.

Murder is as much a part of our world as that of the Old Testament and if two-thousand years of Christianity had done little to eradicate it, it is because we have swopped Christian pharisaism for the Jewish one. Nothing has changed but the words. Terrorism today has exhausted the vocabulary of death to describe the horrific killings of the last decade. But as John Paul II said in Drogheda, 'nobody may ever call murder by any other name than murder.'

Recently, the German Government decided to introduce Peace in Europe as a subject in their secondary schools. The need is that desperate. Reconciliation has to be taught if it is ever to become a reality. The Sign of Peace is a sacrament capable of transforming our worship of God into love of his creatures. In a world where signs of peace are often all too remote, we cannot afford to ignore this little one.

The Master's table

Christ knows our failings and our weaknesses. He knows our troubles better than we do ourselves and He wants to help us. Other people give us a helping hand when we are in trouble. Christ gives us His whole body so that we might borrow His whole might in carrying our burdens. 'This is my body which is given for you,' He said (1 Cor 11:24). It is sad to see how many of us let such help go a-begging. And the real tragedy is that just those people who most need it seldom take it.

People don't seem to realise that Holy Communion is God's way of helping them. I remember a certain man who went to Holy Communion every morning. And the strange thing about this man was that I never saw him outside the church but he was drunk. I was young then, too young to realise that he was an alcoholic. He isn't the type most of us would expect to find at the altar-rails every morning. But he is the type God expects to find there. And he knew that. He pestered heaven with his pleas for help. He put me in mind of the way that Canaanite woman kept nagging at Jesus to cure her little girl. (Oddly enough, this incident is recorded almost immediately before the Feeding of the Four Thousand.) Her insistence was matched only by Christ's indifference: 'He did not answer her a word.' When He did speak it was so unlike him: 'It is not fair to take the children's bread and throw it to the dogs,' he said. But a child's pain can make a mother eloquent and the woman answered Him: 'Even the dogs eat the crumbs which fall from the master's table.' It was enough. Her prayer was answered. Like that woman, and that alcoholic, we too should come for 'the crumbs that fall from the Master's table'. And the greater our needs, the more we should come.

'If I send them away hungry to their homes they will faint on the way; and some of them have come a long way' (Mk 8:3). The way for all of us is hard and for some it is long. If we fall or faint on the way, we have no one to blame but ourselves. Christ doesn't send anyone away hungry.

Good old days

Lady Marjory is serenely elegant in her drawing room upstairs, sipping tea while Mrs Bridges fusses about contentedly downstairs in the kitchen preparing the dinner-menu. Hudson seems to spend most of his time on the stairs moving incessantly between both worlds, changing roles as often as he changes jackets, becoming a servant upstairs and an aristocrat downstairs. It is a world where everybody knows his place and keeps to it. It is a world too very very far removed from our own. And yet *Upstairs, Downstairs* was a surprisingly popular series. Nostalgia has proved to be very much a winner with T.V. programme-makers and don't they know it!

What is there that is so appealing about those former ages? Why should we be so attracted to looking back? Maybe it is that we want to escape the drudgery of the present or more importantly nowadays, the dreadful uncertainties of the future? Or are we trying to find again our lost innocence, that period in our lives when we were totally secure? When we held on to father's hand and father was God almighty to us. Back-to-the-womb, I think psychologists call it. Nostalgia seems to be more prevalent among the old. Perhaps because they have more to look back at than forward to. Or are they afraid to look ahead? Whatever the reasons for it are, many people think the Golden Age is somewhere in the past and unconsciously at least, they yearn for their lost paradise.

I think it is a dangerous thing to over-indulge in nostalgia. First of all, it is pointless – no matter how much we want it, we cannot turn the clock back. Besides, looking back is deceiving. Memory is highly selective. We remember the good times and bury the unpleasant ones. Strange isn't it, how the summers of long ago were all sunshine. Somebody once said, and there is an awful lot of truth in it, that life in every other age was 'nasty, brutish and short'. The great difference between the past and now is that in the old days very few people could afford to do anything and even for the better-off the standard of living was infinitely lower than it is now for everyone. There is an old Russian proverb which says 'Look at the past and you will lose one eye'. We need our two eyes to cope with the present. I suppose that is the worst aspect of it. It's unfair to the present. Nobody ever solved their problem by running home to Mother. It's an illusion to think that old solutions are the answer to modern problems.

Above all, nostalgia is not for Christians. Our religion leads us not back towards a lost paradise but forward towards the Promised Land. We should be looking forward with hope, not back with regret. 'No one who puts his hand to the plough and looks back,' as Christ put it, 'is fit for the Kingdom of God' (Lk 9:62).

Lost opportunities

Most shop assistants become very proficient at recognising this particular type of customer. They come in to buy a pair of shoes, and they just can't make up their minds which pair to buy. They try on one pair after another and when they've gone through the whole range and the shop is littered with boxes, they begin all over again. Anything in the nature of help or advice from the shop assistant is greeted with suspicion. They're being conned. An inferior article or an overpriced one is being dumped on them. No, they'll make up their own minds even if it takes all day. Just when you think they have finally made up their minds they begin to have second thoughts. In the end they leave without buying anything, full of apologies and promises to be back. Nobody could blame a shop-assistant for feeling annoyed and frustrated with such a customer. What we often forget is that those poor unfortunate creatures who couldn't decide about a pair of shoes, go through hell every time they're faced with a decision. They have a morbid dread of making decisions no matter how petty. Psychiatrists call it 'decidophobia'.

At least in the case of the shoes nobody really suffers but the customer himself. This is not true of most decisions we have to make. They affect other people and often very considerably. Many of us end up in some sort of decision-making position in life. When we fail to make decisions we're letting others down. At some stage in our lives, we've all experienced the superior who couldn't make up his mind. Always teetering on the edge of a decision, drawing back at the last moment, dithering indefinitely over minutiae. They make life miserable not only for themselves but for those who work under them. These are times when we are hard put to keep from blurting out: 'For God's sake, make up your mind, it's not the end of the world.' But Nero fiddled while Rome burned and then as now, it is the innocent who suffer.

Some attempt to pass off all this dithering and procrastination as some sort of wisdom. 'Time is a great healer,' says he puffing his pipe. When what he means is a problem shelved is a problem solved. It's extraordinary the effort we make to whitewash our indecisiveness. We pose as traditionalists, we invoke precedents, follow the regulations – anything but make a decision. We drift through life – shelving problems, shirking responsibility, shunning risks, avoiding decision, playing safe by doing nothing. There are always those who will thank us for not rocking the boat – because it leaves them undisturbed in their own little rut. The older we get, the more skilful we become in avoiding decisions. Somebody once said the old don't become wise, they become careful. There's a lot of truth in it.

When we're confessing our sins before Mass, we use the expression 'what we have failed to do'. It covers more of our sins than we imagine. The decisions we failed to make are really opportunities missed, talents wasted, lives blighted, graces denied. Notice how cheerfully children make up their minds with a nursery rhyme – 'eeny, meeny, myny, mo'. 'Unless you become like little children you cannot enter the Kingdom of Heaven.'

I have a dream

Every bullet fired, every bomb exploded, every person killed or maimed in Belfast or Beirut only seems to push further and further away whatever tiny hopes still exist of an eventual settlement. The communities there seem locked in a suicidal struggle in which there can be no victors. Violence is indeed a vicious circle. Reprisal follows reprisal in an orgy of death and blood and destruction. But the most frightening thing of all is the growing number of people who shake their heads and say: 'There's no way out. There's no hope.' Those who have come to accept what the politicians call 'a doomsday situation'. This is frightening. It's the sin of despair, the sin of Judas, the sin against the Holy Spirit, the essence of Hell itself as Dante saw when he inscribed on the gates of Hell: 'Abandon hope all ye who enter here.'

No matter how hopeless things seem, how desperate the situation becomes, we must never lose hope. Because hope is the only way out. It is the light at the end of the tunnel. The alternative to hope is Hell.

The situation in Belfast and Beirut is fairly symptomatic of life in general nowadays. Crisis follows crisis with depressing monotony. Every news bulletin recounts its daily litany of disasters. Statistics record the growing rate of crime, alcoholism, abortion and a host of other disturbing trends. Economic depression, inflation and unemployment contribute to the growing despair in which many people live. Modern man has a morbid fascination for bad news.

Now, more than ever before, the world needs hope. Teilhard de Chardin said: 'The world belongs to him who will give it its greatest hope.' And Vatican II echoed the same thought: 'The future,' it said, 'is in the hands of those who know how to give tomorrow's generations reasons to live and hope.' The great prophets of our time were not prophets of doom but prophets of hope. Men like Pope John and his Council, John F. Kennedy and his New Frontier. Remember his inaugural speech: 'Some men look at things as they are and ask why. I dream of things that never were and ask why not.' And Martin Luther King and his great Civil Rights Crusade: 'I have a dream,' he told his people. 'I have climbed the mountain and I've seen the promised land.' Their lives were cut short by an assassin's bullet but their hopes can never be extinguished.

As Christians we should be in the front ranks of every band of hope and glory, however small. Our religion is founded on hope. 'Thy kingdom come,' we pray in the Our Father. In the May Revolution of '68 the students of Paris carried a banner emblazoned with the words: 'Be reasonable. Ask for the impossible'. And why not? Ours is an impossible dream. But then we follow one who said: 'With me all things are possible.'

Behaviour

A sense of sin

'I wonder, Father, would you have a word with young Jimmy. He hasn't been to confession for a long time.' It is the kind of request many mothers make nowadays when a priest drops in on them. Probably many others don't ask because they have a vague feeling it might only aggravate the situation. They are afraid of giving the impression of interfering in a very personal matter. Waiting for the right moment – which never really comes – the priest broaches the matter with Jimmy. 'I've nothing really to tell,' is Jimmy's answer. Saturday evening's near-empty confessionals suggest that Jimmy is no solitary exception.

There was a time not so long ago when there were long queues outside every box, when priests were inclined to become edgy after long sessions and not above letting the odd roar which was every penitent's greatest fear. What happened to cause such a startling change? Many people found the mechanical nature of the sacrament unacceptable. Rattling off a set list of sins – sins learned to be confessed, rather than those really committed. Old legalism prevailed, with which confessions dealt so admirably, 'I ate meat on Friday' sort of thing. Perhaps, the anxiety to get rid of that and the scruples and the guilt-complexes it spawned, blurred the awareness of sin itself. Perhaps, the baby has been thrown out with the bathwater.

The long confessional queues are no great loss, to penitents no less than to confessors. Something else is. A sense of sin, of personal responsibility for evil. '*I*' must be consciously restored to the centre of sin. As David realised after his torrid fling with Bathsheba, and a finger-pointing session with the prophet, Nathan:

My offences truly I know them, *My* sin is always before me.
Against you, you alone have *I* sinned.
What is evil in your sight *I* have done (Ps 51:3-4).

If we've got nothing really to tell, we've got something really to worry about. Because we've lost our awarness of sin. Without that we can't even begin to find God. David's *Miserere* marked his turning back to God. And remember the Prodigal Son. It was precisely with the words, '*I* have sinned against heaven and against you' that he began his journey back to his father.

I'm the greatest

When Cassius Clay first exploded on the world scene a couple of years ago and proclaimed unashamedly to a dumb-struck public 'I'm the greatest' I think something finally snapped. Our guilt complex about pride. We sniggered a little at first at the Louisville Lip but a couple of knockouts later, we were all ardent fans. Some even now claim the whole affair was a superb confidence trick, that he bamboozled his opponents with bluff, that he literally talked the fight out of them. Certainly, the scornful way he predicted at every weigh-in the knockout round, the disdainful way he treated his opponents, dropping his guard, patting them contemptuously on the head and all the time keeping up a lively commentary for the benefit of the crowd, must have been enough to demoralise any fighter. And of course Cassius won and the world accepted his claim. And swallowed his message too. If you want to be great, you've gotta convince yourself first.

There have been other noteworthy examples besides Cassius in the last decade or two. Certainly more sophisticated, perhaps, less obvious. The arrogance of a man like General Charles de Gaulle, who could say, without batting an eye 'I am France'. And dare I say it – we all have household gods – the youthful pride of J. F. Kennedy, who set out to become President of the U.S. because as he put it 'he was the best man for the job'. And look at the pop scene. The pomposity of a pop-idol like John Lennon who claimed the Beatles were more popular than Jesus Christ. And look at the arrogance of the younger generation! Their contempt for established values; their disdain for tradition, the sheer cockiness of their brave, new world. What a pity such grand idealism should be marred by such gross pride.

In fact, if the modern world has any one outstanding message for us, it is that you can go a long way with a little talent and a lot of neck. And if you can't achieve fame, you can always settle for notoriety. The Guinness Book of Records has a niche to satisfy almost everybody's pride, a place to record even our most uselsss talents. The fact that it is the fastest-selling book second only to the Bible, is itself a significant comment on the world we live in, with its obsession with record-breaking and proliferation of contests of every conceivable sort. The Hall of Fame, it seems, is no longer only for the Greats. There is plenty of room for the near-greats and indeed the not-so-greats.

Pride of birth in former days has given way to pride of achievement in this age. The great goal of life is success. The self-made man is the most admired and if the bottom rung on the ladder of success is self-confidence, self-delusion is surely the top one. At any rate there is no place there for humility and self-effacement is a mortal sin in a world where to get on is the top priority. What then are we to tell our children? 'Son, be a proud man and hold your head up high' as the song has it, or as Christ would have you say: 'Learn of me, for I am meek and humble of heart.' The choice is ours.

The clenched fist

You don't have to look very hard at this world of ours to see that anger is one of the very important ingredients of success. Imagine Ayatollah Khomeini without anger or Ian Paisley, or Angela Davis. Name, if you can, any popular hero of this present age, or for that matter any other age who is not fired by anger. You may have protests without violence but never without anger. Very often the sincerity of one's patriotism is measured by the vehemence of one's anger. And anger is not the property of any one group, though the media often suggest otherwise. For every angry young man, there is an angry old man; for every angry protestor, there is an angry policeman; for every angry leftist there is an angry fascist. The protester often appears as a person spoiling for a fight, when the real culprit is the establishment which burgled his rights. Violence and internment are two sides of the same coin, and that coin is anger. The clenched fist so often succeeds where the olive branch fails.

Outside politics, anger may not be so conspicuous, but make no mistake about it, it is there in a big way. In the superstar world it is a sine-qua-non of stardom. You've never quite made it until you can storm out of La Scala like Maria Callas, or walk off the set like Elizabeth Taylor and that with impunity, in the certain knowledge that the big brass will come crawling to you on its knees to smooth your ruffled feathers. It is what separates John MacEnroe from all the other greats. It is what makes Cassius Clay the greatest. And look at the coverage. You couldn't buy that kind of space any more. The media seems to thrive on anger. It captures the banner headlines. 'Bishop condemns, Minister lashes out, Priest rebukes', What T.V. chat show stands out in your mind? What other except the night the roof fell in and all hell broke loose, with audience and panellists firing insults at each other to beat the band. Does anybody remember now what it was all about?

I suppose the outstanding advantage of anger is that it gets notice, it attracts attention, it gets results. It is probably the first lesson we all learned in the cradle. The bawling baby gets its bottle. Industrial disputes get nowhere until a strike is threatened. Nothing quite perks up the business like firing somebody. It is the most compelling reason put forward for violence. Anger is the attribute of the achiever. Meekness and compassion are only for losers.

The truth as always is simple and startling. Anger solves nothing.

It doesn't take away grievances; it exacerbates them. When the flood of passion has subsided the breaches remain, in fact wider than ever. As the Bible puts it and this is worth thinking about, 'The anger of man does not achieve the justice of God.'

Keeping up with the Jones

In advertising circles they call it creating a need. In plain language it simply means – working up the old jealously angle. In the old days it held its own among the Seven Deadly Sins. There was even a time when people used to confess it – 'I coveted my neighbour's house, Father.' 'Covet' – there is a word that has almost disappeared from the spoken language. And 'jealous' – that is used almost exclusively nowadays about affairs of the heart. But human nature remains the same – human frailty too. To paraphrase an old chestnut – 'old sins never die, they're only phrased away.' And that is what happened to envy. It was given a new label and became respectable. They talk about sex being a great money-spinner, but envy is the life blood of business.

Take the ordinary average middle-class couple. They've got a home and a steady income. A nice comfortable set-up. Some might even think them lucky. But like Adam and Eve in the garden, their troubles are only beginning. And there is no shortage of serpents. The consumer society is riddled with them. And now as then, the major assault is launched on the woman. Rightly or wrongly, society regards her as the weak link. Just look at the fashion industry! Her main anxiety is to keep up appearances. It means a lot of things her mother would have considered unnecessary – wall-to-wall carpeting, central-heating, washing-machine, fridge, deep-freeze, even a couple of antiques. It means giving a few dinner-parties, joining a few clubs, having a continental holiday. The gin-and-tonic society sets ever-rising standards, and keeping-up-with-the-Jones is top priority.

And what about himself? He has got a job with good promotional prospects. He shares an office with another junior executive and has access to the typing-pool. Later if he shows the right attitudes, he will be given an office of his own. Later still he will get his own secretary. He might even end up with a directorship and a suite of offices. In the meantime all he has to do is envy his betters, and work a little harder, join the right clubs, move in the right circles. With the company dangling the carrot in front of him and the little woman cracking the whip behind him there is only one direction he can go – up the ulcer-ridden, nerve-wracking ladder of success.

'They're not typical,' I can see you shaking your head. 'You're reading too many novels, seeing too many films.' Don't fool yourselves, we've joined the queue for the good life, and we're pushing just as hard as anybody else.

Look at our industrial disputes and observe the number of status claims that cause strikes, especially among the blue-collar and white-collar workers. And look at the leap-frogging among the salaried professions. It is not how much you get that seems to matter but how much more than the other fellow. It's holding your place on the league-table that really counts. And what about suburban-life here? Is it significantly different from suburban life in America? Surely the difference between the rat-race here and the rat-race there is simply a matter of degree, a question of opportunity. And we are catching up fast. And what is so wrong about it all? Well, for one thing, it is a question of priorities. Christ said, 'Pagans set their hearts on all these things. Set your hearts on His kingdom first and all these things will be given you as well' (Mt 6:33).

Rags to riches

It is the line usually taken in the success stories of the Sunday news-papers. Every word fairly bleeds with admiration for the hero in the rags-to-riches epics. We are treated to a blow-by-blow account of how he made his first million, all the way from street urchin to ship-building tycoon. Like the old lives of the saints, there is a remarkable similarity in detail in all these epics. They begin with grinding poverty, usually of the barefooted variety; the hero is backward at school and drops out. All dunces take heart! Then he spends a few years in the wilderness, simply dossing. Then it happens! The strange experience, the turning point, the blinding flash of revelation, followed by a life of total dedication to making money. The ending is, of course, pre-sumed happy-ever-after. The account is generously sprinkled with the wise sayings and maxims of these secular saints, for the guidance of those who yearn to scale such heights. Needless to say, there is no mention of shady deals, of colleagues clobbered, of competitors knifed, of employees exploited or of values lost. And of course the question is never asked what is the point of it all? For those who lack the dedication of an Aristotle Onassis or a Nelson Rockefeller, shortcuts to fortune are provided. Admittedly at much longer odds. You could take a chance on winning the sweep or the pools, or even the crosswords or fashion competitions. And if you find yourself becoming depressed at continued failure, then read the stories of the lucky winners and how 'in spite of everything they never lost heart'. And there's nothing like watching 'Jackpot' or 'Take Your Pick' on TV for keeping up the interest. By the way, a little bit of superstition is helpful. Avoid 13s and black cats etc. And of course read your stars. If it doesn't help you win, it at least helps to explain why you are not winning.

Incredible, isn't it, that the virtue which the world encourages us so much to acquire is the sin of avarice. In fact one of the Seven Deadly Sins. The one thing about which Christ was so blunt. 'You cannot serve God and money.' 'It is harder for a camel to pass through the eye of a needle than for a rich man to enter heaven.' And remember the sad fate of the hoarder: 'Fool, this night do I require thy soul of thee.' And the even sadder fate of Judas – and all for a handful of silver. It is no coincidence that when Christ preached his famous Sermon on the Mount he began with the words: 'Happy are the poor, for theirs is the kingdom of God.' And it is not surprising that the

Church, wishing to steer a soul in God's direction always recommended Poverty, Chastity and Obedience – and in that order. Because the very first steps we take towards God must be away from wealth. The hand that reaches out for God must be empty.

The sexual revolution

This, it seems, is the age of revolutions. Ever since the French Revolution, society has been rocked spasmodically by movements, often violent, aimed at overthrowing the *status quo* and inaugurating a brave, new world. They are society's growing pains, evolution by revolution. The latest of these is the 'sexual revolution'. Possibly more ink has been spilt (better ink than blood!) on this one than on many of its noble predecessors. But what is remarkable about it is how society is endeavouring to make a virtue out of what is in fact a vice. How it is trying to make an honest woman out of lust and how far it is succeeding. Whether lust is more prevalent today than ever before is questionable. It has had a pretty consistent record down through the ages; from ancient Rome to modern Sweden. Prostitution is the oldest profession in the world and men indulged in pornography almost before they could write. But what is new, at least on the scale attempted today, is the campaign to make a virtue out of it. And that, more than anything else is what the 'sexual revolution' is all about.

Notice, for example, how it has linked itself to so many of today's worthy causes and how respectable it has become as a result. Take the whole emancipation movement. No woman can be regarded as truly liberated unless she has liberated herself from sexual taboos as well. And what started out as a pots-and-pans revolution easily escalates into a demand for a relaxation of marriage laws. The universal demand for more freedom, more rights for individuals invariably leads to a demand for greater sexual freedom as well. It is significant that the two most publicised questions after Vatican II have probably been contraception for married couples and optional celibacy for the clergy.

And of course, ever since Freud, the language of experts is loaded against the virtuous. The word 'healthy' is now used frequently to denote freedom from guilt-complexes. The person with a conscience is a guilt-ridden neurotic. Self-control is dismissed as sublimation. Virility seems a virtue rather than a biological fact. Chastity is equated with frigidity. And most ironical of all, innocence is used to describe absense of sexual inhibitions. It is not so much what is said as what is insinuated that sows the nagging doubts. Of course, there were a lot of puritanical notions about sex, and probably still are. Freud and others have done an awful lot of good in freeing us from them. But to make freedom out of what is in fact licence and a virtue out of what is in fact a vice will not solve anybody's problems.

Anybody who has any sort of passing acquaintanceship with the Bible could hardly regard it as even mildly puritanical in the matter of sex. Among the many great people whose lives are recorded there, three are outstanding: Samson, for his great strength, Solomon for his wisdom, and David for his holiness. All three failed spectacularly in the matter of sex. Admittedly we have come a long way since then but we should not easily presume ourselves to be stronger than Samson, wiser than Solomon or holier than David.

'If you cannot be good, be careful' used to be a joke directed at courting couples. Recently, it has assumed a sinister new seriousness. Revolutions have a strange predilection for ending in blood-baths. The French Revolution ended in the Reign of Terror, the Russian one, in the Stalinist purges. It seems the 'sexual revolution' is not going to prove an exception. AIDS, like a medieval plague, threatens to sweep across the globe, leaving a trail of death in its wake like the Black Death. Eminent medical experts begin to sound like biblical prophets or Redemptorist preachers, thundering warnings to the sexually promiscuous, of 'the wrath to come'. Chastity might once again become respectable.

Easy Rider

It was extolled by the poets of the beat generation. It was celebrated in the folk-songs of Joan Baez or Tom Paxon. It was glamourised in films like *Easy Rider* or *Midnight Cowboy* or T.V. serials like *Here comes Bronson*. It was raised to the level of a philosophy by a university don like Timothy O'Leary. Some even give it the trappings of religion. But be it fad or philosophy, protest or prank it was the in-thing among the sixties generation. A guitar, a motor-bike, an open road to nowhere. The drop-outs, Paradise. The attitude it represented, the virtue it extolled would seem to be none other than sloth – one-time member of the group known as the Seven Deadly Sins.

But these hippies, the back-to-the-soil romantics, are by no means the only enthusiasts for sloth. It became quite respectable even among 'yuppies'. Except they call it 'getting-away-from-it-all' instead of 'dropping-out'. Holiday brochures offer a wide variety of it from the secluded beach to the Mediterranean cruise. The Saturday-Night-Sunday-Morning has developed into the long weekend. The shorter working hours, the labour-saving gadgetry in the home have created a time-slot in our lives which is being filled more and more by spectator-sports and T.V. watching. It was once fondly thought that modern technology by shortening working hours would leave us free for self-development. Whatever evidence there is suggests that most of us, when we are free, prefer to do nothing.

Work has lost all meaning except as a means of providing the where-withall for leisure. The notion of work as a vocation is fast losing ground. 'Punching-in-time' – we all do more of it than we care to admit. Work-to-rule is not only a strike weapon, it is a permanent way of life with some. Admittedly the drudgery and monotony of many assembly-line jobs make it easier to understand. The mere cog-in-the-wheel feeling is hard to overcome. And pride in one's work is not easy to maintain when one is constantly competing against a machine. The rigid departmentalisation of work especially in larger companies is another factor contributing to sloth. Remember the celebrated case of the liner Queen Elizabeth II. Thousands of men were thrown out of work beause it couldn't be decided whether the moving of a lead pipe from A to B was the work of a fitter or a plumber. 'Sorry it's not my department' is a frequent way of getting rid of an awkward assignment. Other unpleasant matters are 'shelved'. 'Passing the buck' is standard practice. 'Accountability' is to be avoided at all costs. Shoddy workmanship must not be traceable. The complaining customer is a crank. Anyway, what can you expect with conditions like ours and for the sort of money we get?

We spend our working hours waiting for the bell to ring or the whistle to blow. Waiting for the nod to pack up and go. Almost like runners on their marks waiting for the starter's pistol. Only then do we start living. But we can't compartmentalise our lives. We were created in the image of our Maker. We were designed to share in His creativity. When we shirk our work we spit in His eye.

The Bible puts it briefly and bluntly:

He who is slack in his work
is a brother to him who destroys (Prov 18:9).

The battle of the bulge

When I was at boarding-school, my greatest obsession was food. I used to dream about finding roast-chickens or apple-tarts when I lifted the lid of my desk in class or opened my locker in the dormitory. I waited in mouth-watering anticipation for every visiting day, wondering what goodies it might bring. I can still remember vividly the ecstasy experienced by the sight of a lone sausage on a plate for tea. My most abiding memory of the seminary is the whiff of a fry from the professors' refectory as we headed in for our plate of porridge in the mornings. No more sophisticated torture has ever been conceived. Having survived that, I think I can survive anything. Those were the days when I could fully appreciate Christ's description of heaven as a banquet, as I imagine would most of the starving people of the Third World today. I don't think it has much appeal in the West nowadays. And I think that's understandable.

Over-indulgence is a way of life with us. Eating has become almost a burden. People actually complain about having to attend a dinner, having to entertain clients. And no wonder! Leaving aside for the moment the three or four regular meals which we are burdened with, the in-between-meal consumption is enormous. Coffee-break at 11 o'clock, four o'clock tea and a light supper at bed-time. The bag of chips, the potato-chips, the chocolates, the fruit, the ice-cream and of course the drink, make a staggering total. Take a stroll through a bingo-hall after a session is over. The incredible amount of litter there makes you wonder whether the people came for the bingo or for the grub. In fact, one of the by-products of all this excessive eating is the litter problem. Futurists warn us that some day we may be in danger of being buried beneath our own litter. In the old days, the trouble of preparing food and the burden of cleaning up afterwards acted as a check on our gluttonous instincts. But nowadays, with instant foods, T.V. dinners, and the throw-away containers, these restraints have gone.

Strangely enough, of all the Seven Deadly Sins, gluttony alone is still regarded by the world as a mortal sin – not because it kills the soul but because it kills the body. The preachers of this world warn us solemnly – we are eating, drinking, smoking and drugging ourselves to death. The evils in store for the gluttons are luridly depicted. Every 30 seconds a European dies of heart-failure caused by over-indulgence. The collapsed kidney of the alcoholic and the cancer-eaten lung of the cigarette-addict are displayed as evidence of the wrath to come from our excesses. Hell fire was never plugged like this. And the message is being received loud and clear. Conversions are rising rapidly. Look at the swelling numbers of the calorie-conscious people, the weight watchers. Dieting is one of the fastest growing businesses. The battle of the bulge, the fight against flab is on. Ironically enough, these very people for whom fasting as self-denial was an intolerable burden have become the most avid diet enthusiasts. And no fast ever imposed by religion could match the severity of these self-imposed diets. And for what? – to take inches off a waist or even for that matter to add a few years to a life? So much energy for such small returns. It is a pity we don't channel all this wonderful enthusiasm into some really worthwhile cause like saving our souls.

Runs in the family

Suddenly you become aware of the woman opposite signalling frantically with her eyes. Or you are brought up sharply by a warning kick under the table or a pinch in the arm or a jab in the ribs. Or perhaps you get a tip-off when you arrive. You are cornered for a moment early on and given the score. What is all the big sweat about? Well, it seems that in the present company certain topics could ruin the whole evening. Because when they are mentioned, the boss, the host, father or Uncle Tom throws a fit. And there is always a little wife whose main task in life is to keep her husband's blood pressure down. So for her sake, you join the conspiracy for one more evening in your life. I remember arriving one Summer to do a supply in a city parish in New York. As I was going in to the dining-room for the evening meal, I was drawn aside by one of the young priests and given a friendly word of advice: 'Don't mention the war in Vietnam or contraception or drugs or the negro question.' Apparently the pastor got worked up when these were mentioned. 'What should I talk about?' I asked. 'Stick to baseball,' he said, 'it's pretty safe.' So I had baseball for dinner for two months. Well, the boss is the boss. And of course, we are all naturally more sensitive and diplomatic when it is the boss who has the prejudice. If he happens to be a subordinate we can occasionally take pleasure in knocking a rise out of him.

I think it was Einstein who said: 'It is easier to split the atom than destroy a prejudice.' I never realised how true that was until I tried to teach the Civil War to a class of 17 year olds. They were almost every bit as fiercely partisan as their grandfathers were when they fought it 60 years ago. And then since the Troubles in the North began you cannot be sure even of your best friend any more. Isn't it remarkable how the voice hardens, the neck swells, the face reddens and the eyes bulge as we launch into a tirade about the British Army or the I.R.A. or the Orange Order. What began as a friendly discussion suddenly degenerates into a brawl. Prejudice, like Original Sin 'clouds our minds, darkens our understanding and makes us prone to evil'. The Creation story makes the devil the father of prejudice when he poisoned Eve's mind and she in turn poisoned Adam's.

I used to think once that education was the answer. In theory it is, but not always in practice. As my mother used to say to my father after some little tiff – he was a schoolteacher: 'There is nobody as

127

ignorant as an ignorant schoolteacher.' The trouble, of course, with education, and this applies even more to the home than the school, children are sometimes taught *what* to think rather than *how* to think. The sight of a father letting off steam about politics or religion at the dinner table in front of his children would be funny if it weren't so tragic. Children are very impressionable. Their father is a God-figure to them. He is always right. They are not capable of filtering fact from fiction, truth from falsehood. They should not be exposed to the emotional outbursts of adults, especially if they happen to be their parents. Their minds are easily warped when they are young, not so easily straightened out when they are older. And one of the extraordinary things about prejudices is that they do seem to run in families.

The definition of an educated man I like best is 'one who can argue with his fellowman without quarrelling'. Not a bad defninition of a Christian either. We might make a start by accepting that we are all to some extent prisoners of prejudice, and that, as the Bible puts it: 'only the truth can make us free.'

Law-abiding

There is always that lip-biting before going to the altar-rails to receive Holy Communion. If you are a routine person you can tick sins off like a shopping-list. Or maybe you haven't a list? You probably have just one big doubt, the great lonely question which plagues most of us: Did I consent? And sin or at least, mortal sin, is that confused mess of thoughts, temptations, deeds and dreams of sex.

If that is your experience, and it would console me to think it is, then the Gospel should be an eye-opener to you. If you have doubts before receiving, they should be centred on love, not on law, on charity, not on chastity. It is very easy to slip into worrying about the laws you have broken and contenting yourself with legal cleanness. This was the 'righteousness of the Pharisses' which Jesus detested so much.

'If you remember that your brother has anything against you.' It is amazing how weak our memories can be in this area. All the more amazing because this is the area in which we really live. Your brother – your family, your mother-in-law, your father-in-law, your employer, employee, neighbour, rival, mate. And your special pain-in-the-neck. Don't bother to list *your* grievances now. Think about *his*. They are your real sins. Sometimes in our anxiety to remember the sins we were taught about we overlook the ones we really commit.

If ever you should be reconciled with your brother, Communion is the time for it. There is no point in carrying your grudges up to the altar-rails with you. Your brother is the only image you have of God, poor though he may be. You cannot love God and hate him. If you say so you are a liar. And there can be no real communion between you and God. The only way Communion can bring God into our lives and make this world more tolerant and more tolerable is by ridding ourselves of that hypocrite who struts about so smugly in our shoes.

Weeding Out

As any gardener knows, weeding can be the greatest threat of all to the life of the young seedling. At first, the problem is one of identification. The weeds must be left until the seedling can be clearly recognised. Even then, removing the weeds may pose an even greater threat. It might sever the seedling's root system. In the case of human beings it is an even more hazardous occupation. The fact that 'weeding-out' as a means of solving problems has no history of success, does not seem in the least to curb man's passion for it. Hitler's final solution, the great weeding-out of six million Jews in concentration camps like Dachau and Auswitz, is quickly forgotten. Race, religion, colour, sex, politics, wealth continue to be a convenient sort of ready-reckoner for identifying weeds. Man's increasing power over nature has provided him with new and sinister instruments for weeding-out. The unborn child, the seed of life, is now threatened by abortion. At the other end of life, euthanasia is proposed as the final solution for the new Jews – the old, the maimed, the incurables and the burdensome. And right through life, the weeding-out continues remorselessly. The handicapped are institutionalised, the delinquent is penalised, the poor are patronised and the deviant is ostracised.

But the weeding-out is not confined to faceless bureaucracy. We've all tried our hand at it. And we like to think our judicious weeding-out prevented many great personal calamities. We are very sharp at spotting the undesirables, the troublemakers, the misfits. We may admit reluctantly to lapses in our watchfulness but never to mistakes.

One shudders to think of the people who might have been weeded-out if men had got their way and God himself had not chosen to intervene. That rabble-rouser, Jesus Christ, if Caiphas and his cronies had their way, and Peter after his triple denial in the crucifixion crisis should have been weeded-out for failing in the leadership test. Strange isn't it, that Christ never weeded-out Judas? The Church's own record of weeding-out showed little of her master's tolerance. The Inquisition has never been surpassed as a weeder. Galileo could testfy to that. Excommunications and anathemas may be out of fashion but old habits die hard.

The lesson of the parable of the weeds is so uncompromisingly simple and so widely ignored. To the question 'Do you want us to go and weed it out?' the answer is a categorical 'No.' And the reason is self-evident. Only God has eyes sufficiently discerning and fingers sufficiently gentle for this job. Weeding-out is God's prerogative. Life would be so much better for everybody, if only we would leave it to him.

Society

For Evil to Triumph

When I was going to school the swish of a cane was just as familiar a sound as the school-bell is now. Looking back it seems that somebody was always being slapped. You could never really feel safe. In fact the most dangerous time was when teacher left the room for some reason or other. There were always those who felt secure enough then to let a few roars or indulge in a bit of horse-play. The racket would end abruptly when teacher marched in. But the damage was done. Depending on how energetic he felt, teacher would thrash the whole class or else make an example of the front seat or the back seat or some other seat. The satisfaction we got from seeing the goody-goodies getting punished helped to compensate for the pain we felt. Mind you, it didn't seem unjust at all, at the time, that the innocent should be punished equally with the guilty. We probably never heard of the expression 'collective responsibility' but we certainly accepted the principle of it.

Corporal punishment is gone now and I'm afraid collective responsibility has gone with it. Everybody is so insistent nowadays on the rights of the individual that they're inclined to forget their obligation to the community. If things are wrong we must all share the blame. 'It's none of my business' we're inclined to say. The publicans serve drink to teenagers, and the bingo-halls sell tickets to children. Cinemas seem quite content to advertise their films as over 18s only and then admit those who are obviously under that age. The cynical indifference of some is frightening – those who actually employ children in places where the law does not permit them to be. To treat the law with that sort of contempt is asking for trouble. We shouldn't be so surprised when these young people in turn show scant respect for it.

As for the rest of us – our record in this matter is nothing to be proud of. 'For evil to triumph, it's enough that good men do nothing.' But that's not us. We do our bit – we like to think. We show our disapproval, of course. We shake our heads, and tut-tut to each other and make comments under our breath about 'what is the world coming to at all' – when we're confronted by some flagrant breach of conduct on the part of the young. But tut-tutting scarcely fulfils

132

our obligation. We might even throw in a few sharp comments about their parents or teachers or the guards. But collective responsibility means more than merely 'passing the buck'. It may even at times mean confronting the young offenders. If we don't, it's not because we suffer from physical cowardice, but moral cowardice. We're afraid 'it mightn't be good for our business' or most despicable of all, it might make us appear 'squares'.

And all the time what we're really doing is letting down young people by failing to check them. Children are constantly exploring the frontiers of the permissible. They tend to go as far as they're allowed. They depend on us to stop them going over the brink. As somebody once put it, 'There are no delinquent children, really, only delinquent adults.'

The buck stops here

President Truman had a card on his desk in the White House with the words inscribed on it in bold capitals 'The buck stops here'. There is a sort of 'Trumania' I believe, sweeping the U.S. at the moment. Not very greatly admired in his own time, coming as he did between the great Roosevelt and the war-hero Eisenhower, he has become something of cult-figure at the present time. He was a simple ordinary guy with no particular charisma – a man nobody ever expected to become President, still less a good president. He was noted only for plain talking and doing what he thought ought to be done. Incidentally, it was he who ordered the dropping of the atom bomb on Hiroshima and Nagasaki. Not the sort of man really one would expect to be revered posthumously.

But he had what I think is singularly lacking in the present generation – the ability to exercise authority and accept the consequences. He did not shirk his responsibility; he did not 'pass the buck' because he accepted that there was a point where the buck stops and he was that point. In these permissive times, everybody wants to shirk the exercise of authority. People want the privileges of power without the penalties. They avoid making decisions; they are terrified of making mistakes. They have even invented an elaborate ritual to conceal the fact that, most of the time, they are doing nothing. More surveys, in-depth studies, further investigations and above all more committees and more reports – white papers and green papers and blue prints. But no decisions.

From bosses to bishops, from politicians to policemen, from parents to teachers, 'passing the buck' is rampant. Take teenage-drinking. The parents blame the publicans and the schools; the schools blame the parents and the police; the police blame the parents and the publicans. The public generally blames the government and the government commissions a report. Meanwhile the teenagers continue to drink and teenage alcoholism is officially designated a problem area. It is a vicious circle – a very vicious one in this case.

Whatever else you may think of Harry S. Truman, we could all profitably adopt his motto. It would sit as well on a teacher's desk in the class-room as in the headmaster's office; in the priest's parlour as in the Bishop's palace. It would fit indeed anywhere men are 'their brother's keeper'. But nowhere would it fit better nowadays than on the kitchen mantlepiece, with its four simple words pointing straight at us like an accusing finger – 'The buck stops here'. For those of us who have others in our care, our main concern should not be to be popular but to help. And we help most by accepting our responsibility.

No boundaries

I don't know what impact Jimmy Carter made as president of the United States, still less what his place in history will be. But for me if he never did anything else except make the question of human rights a central issue, he will have justified his election. There has always been tremendous complacency on the question of human rights. People feel that it is only a problem in far distant places which are not yet quite civilised and that as those places emerge into the 20th century the problem will disappear. But this view does not tally with the facts. A recent report by Amnesty International states that two-thirds of member states of the United Nations are guilty of major breaches of human rights, like torture, killing and imprisonment. There is almost no country, no government whose hands are completely clean. Only the names change – some call it special powers or emergency measures.

Human rights has always been a great subject for lofty declarations, full of noble sentiments and stirring words. Every modern constitution has its declaration of the rights of man. And as if that were not enough we are now drawing up international charters of human rights at Helsinki, Belgrade and elsewhere. But getting those lofty statements translated into practice is quite another story. Especially as they always insist on inserting the protective clause about non-interference in the internal affairs of member states. And that in a context where two-thirds of them are guilty. It is here, I think, Carter made his great contribution when he declared: 'Human rights have no national boundaries.'

But we all have our own unwritten self-protective clauses. Human rights is always a stick to beat the other fellow with. Trade unions are very insistent on their right to picket. They are not so understanding of the individual's right to pass their pickets and are quick to label those who exercise such a basic human right scabs and blacklegs. Management likes to wax eloquent on the rights of free enterprise but doesn't hesitate to discriminate against those workers they label agitators and trouble-makers. We all agree on itinerants' right to proper housing but not next door to us. There are many husbands who crusade for equal rights from the State for their working wives. They don't always show the same concern for the equal rights of these same wives within the home.

If we want to help others achieve their human rights, we must be credible. We must first put our own house in order. 'The price of freedom is eternal vigilance.' The greatest contribution you and I can make to human rights is to be vigilant in our own backyards. When we have achieved it there, it will have ceased to be a problem elsewhere.

No charge

When my father died some years ago, it fell to me as the only son to look after the affairs of the family as my mother was not too well at the time. My father had retired a short time previously and was in receipt of a government pension. I'll never forget the shock I got when I was officially informed that his pension would cease forthwith. What appalled me then was that my mother was literally cut off without a shilling as a result of my father's death. Had it happened the other way round, had my mother died first, my father would have continued to receive his pension. I think that was the moment of truth for me. That was the moment that decisively converted me to women's rights. I never thought of my father and mother as anything but a unit, a sort of limited company. Whatever contribution my father made in over 50 years service to the State was only possible because my mother looked after his home and raised his children for him. It all seemed so unjust at the time.

A document from the French Hierarchy suggests not state pensions, but state salaries for mothers. And why not? Why should we be so appalled at the idea of mothers getting a salary. After all the State gives allowances for children and even pays the unemployed. Some people feel that it would in some way cheapen motherhood to suggest a salary. But then we pay our doctors and even our priests. And we can even justify it from Scripture. 'The labourer is worthy of his hire.' If priests, why not mothers?

Apart from the justice of the matter, the suggestion does seem to have at least some practical advantages. Most people would concede, I think, that full-time mothers could provide a better home life for children. Running a home and having a job is more than many people are capable of. Both may suffer in consequence. Both Church and State attach great importance to the family and the place of the mothers in it. Mouthing fine phrases is all very well but I think they should work out the Christian implications of these statements. In the present depression, everybody is worried about the lack of job-opporutnities for school-leavers. I don't believe that the retention of married women at work is the primary cause. But if more wives and mothers chose to make a career out of home-making, it would open the job-market for the young. Above all, it is not fair to mothers that they should have to go out to work to maintain or improve their standard of living. If they were paid for being mothers, they would be in a better position to make a choice. The present position is simply unfair.

There is a record called 'No Charge'. It ends with the line 'When it's all added up, the cost of a mother's love is no charge.' And it is true. A good mother is priceless. But that is no reason why we should take them for granted and exploit their generosity and love as we often do.

Rich man's club

Today's world could be divided into those who are dying of mal-nutrition and those who are dying of over-indulgence. And the real scandal is that the Christian religion is heavily concentrated in that area known as the rich man's club. More importantly, it was not nature that bestowed her largess so bounteously on the Christian West. Her industrial might was created out of colonial exploitation and continues to be nourished on cheap raw materials from the Third World. Sharing our bread with the hungry in the poorer parts of this planet is nothing more than simple restitution.

Homelessness is no longer confined to the poor and destitute. Rocketing house prices, uncontrolled land speculation and inept Government planning is causing homelessness in epidemic propor-tions. Young couples are being compelled to mortgage their lives to ensure a roof over their heads. The growing breakdown in family life is not always the fault of modern permissiveness but of inadequate housing. Property speculators cover many categories and most of them are churchgoing Christians. Either the Gospel's cry to shelter the homeless is not relayed in our churches or else it falls on deaf ears.

Nakedness comes in many forms, as many as there are forms of deprivation. A person without a job is naked. The ever-lengthening dole-queue is a line of naked people. The inadequately schooled child is stripped of a decent future. The abandoned old face death stripped of any human comfort. The Gospel's call to clothe the naked is a call to wrap the uncared for in human warmth and concern.

There remains what must be done away with before Christianity becomes a reality, and first among these is the yoke. Christ castigated the Pharisees for placing burdens on other men's shoulders. We live in a very pharisaical world where exploitation comes in striped suits and boardroom talk of cash-flow and profit-margins. Recession becomes an excuse for rationalisation. The workers are not fired, they are laid off. They exchange the yoke of underpayment for that of unemployment.

The clenched fist has been revived in recent times as the symbol of the terrorist, the freedom fighter, the neo-Nazi and even the civil righter. The Red Hand of Ulster has become the clenched fist of the Provisional I.R.A. For the Christian, the clenched fist must be prised open into the hand of friendship.

Inciting to hatred has become so common that it figures today in most countries' statute-books. The wicked word begets bias and prejudice, discrimination and terrorism and eventually war. The word for a Christian is the Word made flesh, Jesus Christ and his all embracing love.

'In this way, your light must shine in the sight of men so that seeing your good works they may give praise to your Father in heaven.'

Behind bars

I spent some time in New York working in a big city parish. One day I got a telephone call to bring Communion to a woman who was sick. She was living in one of these very modern high-rise flats right in the heart of the city. I took the elevator to the sixth floor, worked my way through a maze of corridors and finally found the right number. I rang the bell and the first thing I noticed was an eye staring at me through a peep-hole in the door. Then a voice came over the intercom asking me to identify myself. 'I'm the priest,' I said. 'I was sent for.' Then I heard locks turn, bolts being drawn, and chains being unlocked and finally the door opened to reveal a frightened little woman in her mid-fifties. It was only when I was leaving again that I noticed the inside of the door. It was literally covered from top to bottom with bolts, locks, chains and other security gadgets. No prison-cell ever had so many locks. And when I left I could hear my frightened little friend locking herself in again.

I was talking to a young girl one evening in Paris. When she was leaving, she began by putting on a wind-cheater, scarf and big leather gloves. Then she donned her goggles and her crash-helmet. 'What's all that gear for?' I asked. 'You don't ride a motor-bike?' 'I know,' she said. 'But it makes me look like a boy and I feel safer that way.' I remember recounting this to some Irish girls, and their comment was: 'Don't be talking about Paris, Father. Dublin is every bit as bad.' And one of them added: 'I was attacked one day at eight o'clock in the morning going to work.'

With all the talk about Women's Lib and equal rights for women – and a lot of it is just talk yet – women are still a long way from being equal. And even if we do give them equal pay and equal rights – and mind you, we are doing an awful lot of humming and hawing about it – they still won't have half the God-given rights we are all entitled to, like the right to walk the streets unmolested or to live a normal life free of fear. The plight of women living alone is a special one. Some women remain single by choice, others are victims of circumstances, sometimes heroic. There are in Britain 300,000 spinsters who have chosen this in order to look after their ailing parents. While we cannot guarantee anybody complete protection against the criminal elements in society, we could lift some of the intolerable taboos we have placed on the single woman. Bachelors are immensely better off. They don't have fear to cope with as well as loneliness. They can always shrug off their loneliness by dropping into the nearest pub. Society frowns on the single girl if she goes anywhere alone, except to the shop or to the church.

It is remarkable how much Christ concerned himself during his life with single women. One of the first to greet him in this world was the 84-year-old widow Anna and the first to see him after his Resurrection was Mary Magdalen. And then of course there was his special relationship with the two sisters Martha and Mary which in the end was to cost him his life. We who profess to be Christian should show a little of that great concern Christ had for the single woman.

The games grown-ups play

'To tell the truth, the whole truth and nothing but the truth.' Such is demanded of us in a court of law. But in everyday life we often settle for less – much, much less. But we don't call them lies anymore. We've become too sophisticated for that. Between States we call it 'propaganda' and the irony of that is that the word 'propaganda' originated in the Church. It originally meant the propagation of the faith, the spreading of the Gospel. 'Indoctrination' is another word associated with the modern State and it, too, has its origins in religion. Not only do States have to deceive each other from time to time, governments, too, have to deceive their people occasionally. This is done by 'slanting' – issuing statements which give the 'official slant'. Between political parties it is called the 'party-line'. And 'toeing the party-line' is raised to the level of a virtue. But it doesn't make life any easier for politicians. They are relentlessly pursued by those 'watch-dogs of the public', the high-minded journalists, the skilled interviewers. Their aim is to 'get at the truth'. 'Trial by press' or 'TV ordeal' are the usual methods they employ. But they, too, can have their angles. A good newspaper story is tested by sales, a TV show by Tam-ratings. Controversy makes good TV. Headlines sell newspapers. And the truth can often be so dreadfully dull. So a little 'editing' is always helpful. All this, of course, is done in the 'interests of the public'. The aim of those who 'hold a brief for the public' is to 'create a discerning public', that is, people who can 'read between the lines', or who can easily recognise circumlocution; who can know when the interviewee is 'avoiding the issue', or 'hedging his remarks', or 'choosing his words carefully' to avoid 'alienating public opinion'. Judicious selection of facts and the manipulation of figures are stock in trade to anybody engaged in public life or involved in the communications industry. And the purpose of such ploys is, sometimes, not so much to elucidate the truth as to hide it.

All very complicated, isn't it? But not nearly so dreadful as it might seem. We, the public, have lost our innocence a long time ago. We've grown up in a consumer society and in that world the only thing that is becoming cheaper is the printed and the spoken word. We've grown accustomed to 'sales talk', the 'hard sell' and the 'soft sell', the 'big package', the 'small print'. It's very much a world where to tell the truth is difficult, the whole truth, dangerous and nothing but the truth, downright disastrous.

If these are the games we grown-ups play, what then are we to tell our children? 'Tell the truth and shame the devil?' I think we will have to come up with something better than this, or else accept the generation gap and be prepared for ever-widening generation gaps in the future. Why else do teenagers reject their parents as hypocrites if not because their parents set one standard for themselves and another for their children? This 'credibility' gap is the price we pay for all this devaluation of the spoken and printed word. People don't believe their leaders, students their teachers or children their parents. The disillusionment of youth with the establishment should not be all that surprising in a world which places so little value on truth.

And people complain of a strange new complex – 'loss of identity'. Is it any wonder that people who spend so much time 'creating an image' of themselves for others should forget who they really are? Thomas More was sent to prison for refusing to take the Oath of Supremacy. And while he was awaiting his execution, his wife and daughter came to visit him. They begged him to take the Oath and return home. When he refused they couldn't understand why. He said: 'When a man takes an oath, he places himself in the cup of his hands. If what he swears is false he opens wide his fingers and lets himself slip through, and he may never find himself again.' To More loss of life was preferable to loss of identity. He realised something many of us have forgotten. A man is as good and only as good as his word. The bible puts it: 'He keeps his life who guards his mouth.'

Big Brother is watching

Well, Watergate is gone, but not forgotten. Newspapers have had to look elsewhere for headlines. But before it all disappears into the pages of history, I think there is a lesson there for all of us. It has to do with privacy. Watergate began with a break-in and it ended with a disclosure. If there was one victim more than another – and there were an awful lot of victims – it was not Nixon, it was privacy – the individual's right to privacy.

Recently, in the United States, a scientist demonstrated for me a project he was working on. He showed me an aerial photograph. In one corner there were a few cars driving along the road. They were mere specks. He asked me to pick out one of them and then he proceeded with powerful electronic lens to zone in on this car and blow it up. When he was finished, I could see everything in the car including the driver who was scratching his nose. It was very impressive, but I was more frightened than impressed. Frightened of the ability of modern science to shatter our privacy. In the last decade, two presidents, one in France, the other in America, began their presidencies by promising to stop bugging. These promises themselves are an ominous sign of the times.

Invasion of privacy takes many forms – the TV cameras zoning in on the old lady shuffling down the street, newspaper reporters nosing out the sensational, advertising through the mail, surveys for scientific studies, etc. The arguments put forward for them seem pretty convincing. They are in the interests of the public, in the interests of more authentic documentaries, better news or scientific knowledge. But the end does not jusify the means.

These are the more public forms and therefore the less dangerous. And if there are low standards in this matter in high places, it is probably because there are not very high standards in low places. So look in your own cupboard and see how you indulge your curiosity. Perhaps you don't go around peeping through keyholes or eavesdropping outside doors. Maybe you are not a window-squinter or small-town gossip or anonymous letter writer. It is just that you like to check up on people – people like your employers, your neighbours, even your own children. And you are shocked when your eldest daughter wants to move out because she says 'she has no life of her own'. All you ever did to her was ask her to account for her movements the previous night. Or maybe you went through her purse or read her diary or a letter from her boy-friend. It was only for her own good you were doing it. That is more or less what Nixon said. But the end does not justify the means. Curiosity may or may not have killed the cat but it certainly loses friends, poisons relationships and sows distrust even among families.

Poor visibility

There were many things he was aware of though he had never seen them. He heard words spoken in anger. He felt the pain of them. He could sense the cruelty behind them. But he had never seen the curl of the lip, the glint in the eye, the derangement of the person consumed by hatred. Seeing adds a horror-dimension to what is merely sensed. In time he would learn to recognise with new eyes old acquaintances. he would see and identify the faces of anger, hatred, prejudice, injustice, spite. He who was blind would see the blindness of rage, the blinkered eyes of unjustice, the distorted vision of prejudice, the microscopic stare of fanaticism. The man in the trench coat with the parcel under his arm, 'You have three minutes to clear the hotel before the gelignite goes off,' he informs the receptionist. What does he see? He sees with a blinding lucidity the sanctity of his own cause. He sees nothing else.

Now he would see men close their eyes. He must have often wondered what kind of man used to pass him by, unseeing, as he sat there begging. He could see him now. No monster really. A fairly ordinary individual, obsessed by his own private world, shut in upon himself, blind to the needs of those around him. He would see people close their eyes to the misfortune of others. Or blindfold themselves with platitudes about idleness and the corruption of the dole. And they couldn't see that these poor wretches yearn for health not handouts, work not welfare, a little of the light and warmth of a place in the sun out of the long cold shadow of poverty.

He would see others groping desperately to escape their misery up blind alleys of drink, drugs and sex. He would see them seek blindness because they couldn't bear to look at reality. The depths of unhappiness of those who sought temporary relief in blindness. The sad, sordid fun-places of life with the blind drunk on the pavements, the staring protruding eyes of the drug-addict on his trip, the averted eyes of two strangers coupling in a brothel.

When Christ opened his eyes it was to the blindness of those who had sight. Their great misfortune and ours too, is that we think we see. If only we could admit our blindness and pray that we may see. Our blindness remains only because we haven't the honesty to admit it and the humility to ask for light. 'Lord, that I may see.' It was enough from a blind man. It would be enough from us. Miracles are made from prayers like these.

The end does not justify the means

'It is all in a good cause.' It is amazing how often nowadays you hear that expression. And invariably, you are expected to smile benevolently, and condone whatever bit of hookery is going on. As long as it is all for the good of the company or union, the party or movement it is alright. Your conscience is clear. No sense in quibbling about petty infringements, sharp-practices or shady deals. 'It's all in a good cause.' It is frightening how acceptable that principle – that the end justifies the means – has become, right across the entire spectrum of life.

Take business. Profit justifies everything. It is the name of the game. Whatever makes the till ring is good. It justifies misleading advertising, exploitation, sharp practice. All that matters is that the company is served. Company loyalty is virtue number one and 'I'll scratch you if you scratch me' is the First Commandment. And things on the other side of the fence are not so edifying either. Unions set their own rules. A sort of Robin Hood morality – rob the rich to help the poor. All sorts of dubious practices are justified as long as it is for the workingman. Take strikes. As long as the cause is just the rest of the community can be held up to ranson. A small key industry can blackmail the entire community. It all depends on your economic muscle. Might is right as long as yours is the hand on the lever. There is only one mortal sin and that is passing pickets. Intimidation of individuals is justified in the interests of worker solidarity.

So much for business. What about politics? Here the good of the party seems to be what determines right from wrong. Patronage and pull are justified as serving the interest of the party. Splitting the party is the only unforgiveable sin. And the state itself likes to think it is above party. It sometimes acts as though it were above morality as well. Individual rights and liberties are whittled away on all sorts of important sounding pretexts. Internment is justified on the grounds of law and order. Invasion of privacy on the grounds of national security. At the other end of the scale, subversives seem to have devised a whole system of morality based on the principle that the end justifies the means. For them the end is the Cause with a capital C. As long as 'it's for the Cause', it is alright be it indiscriminate bombing or murder or knee-capping or any of the other unspeakable crimes they indulge in.

But the end does not justify the means. Good motives do not make wrong things right. Was it Danton who said 'Liberty, what terrible crimes have been committed in your name.' Liberty, I think, is only one of a host of good causes for which all sorts of crimes are committed and worse still, condoned.

Environment

The writing on the wall

Driving through a small town recently I couldn't help noticing scrawled on a wall the words 'We want a swimming-pool'. Disfiguring walls seems to be an accepted way for some to parade their grievances. It is certainly eye-catching. Suppose we were all encouraged to scrawl our grievances on the nearest wall. They'd make very interesting reading, especially for others. It might even help to open our eyes to the enormity of other peoples' needs.

'We want a house' would be the plea of an under-privileged family cooped up in a two-roomed tenement. It would express the need too of many better-off newly-weds watching their savings being drained away week after week in rent. 'We want a family' would cover the walls surrounding orphanages with their seven-year-olds condemned to a life in an institution. And the exact same words might be scrawled on the gable-end of a nice suburban semi-detached, where a lonely couple face the bleak prospect of no family of their own. Hospital walls would be covered with the cries of the sick. And cancer wards the desperate pleas of the condemned. The tombstones of young fathers needlessly slaughtered on the roads or in the North would bear the simple inscription 'We want you back'. Railway stations would be covered with 'We want to stay at home' – the last words of departing emigrants. And the walls of Homes with the despair of the inmates: 'We want our children to look after us'; 'We want peace' would cover what walls the bombs have still left standing in Belfast or Beirut. And there are some who are so desperate that all they'd write on the wall would be the one word 'Help!'

And then, of course, the political slogans which now disfigure many of our walls and some of our minds would almost disappear altogether. There would not be much space left for them after people had expressed their real needs. Patriotism is the prerogative of the warm and the well-fed. The poor are devoured by more immediate needs.

Then there are all the other things we would like to have if we had fairy godmothers with magic wands – like swimming-pools. But space would be a problem. There is a limit to what our walls can take. And honestly, I don't believe we would write anything on the wall when the brush is put in our hands except perhaps the one word 'Thanks'. Or perhaps 'Vive moi!' (Hurrah for me!) which Seán Ó Faoláin copied from a wall in the Latin Quarter of Paris. After we had read what others need, we would be too ashamed to ask for more. What happened to the shoe-less beggar would probably happen to us. He went around feeling very sorry for himself because he had no shoes, until he met another beggar who had no feet.

Kilroy was here

He was always one step ahead of the posse. And there he remains, because he strikes only the lonely places in the quiet hours. Darkness is his shield and property his victim. He leaves a trail of maimed objects in his wake. There is no artistry in his touch but he is thorough. What he puts his hand to is irreparably destroyed. And there are no witnesses of his crimes, because the creatures he assaults have no eyes, though their bent and broken remains cry out to heaven for vengeance. We have no description of him; no motive to explain his senseless violence. He circulates freely within the gates. We've passed him many times in the street but never recognised him. Yet, whenever we visit the scene of his crime we know beyond doubt that 'Kilroy was here'. And we know, too, that whatever else he is, he is a very small man with a very big grudge.

Vandalism is accepted in this country, almost as part of the natural order of things. Boys will be boys. Youth must have its fling. The high spirits of youth inevitably leave a trail of devastation in their wake. We've grown accustomed to the broken sign-post, the wrecked telephone-booth, the crushed litter-bin. And public toilets! There has always been a strong body of opinion that felt we are not quite ready for them yet. Anywhere they have been provided, the evidence seems to favour that view. Whatever else they may be called in their present state 'modern conveniences' is certainly a misnomer. Dance-halls, community rooms, waiting-rooms, bus-shelters, park-seats, sea-front dressing-rooms, football-stands, clubhouses – the list is endless. All have been visited by Kilroy and all carry the unmistakable signs of his visits. The newest comers to the list are the school buses. No place is sacred. The pen-knife carvers have long been at work on church seats. Presumably during Mass. Possibly in retaliation for an unduly long sermon.

Attitudes to vandalism vary from mild disapproval to sheer apathy. 'There are more important things to worry about' is the typical re-action of most of us. Explanations for it are plentiful. 'Psychologically, petty vandalism serves as a safety-valve for pent-up repressions, a healthy and harmless way of letting-off steam. Beats war, riots and criminal violence.' So it is argued. If we had to choose between war and smashed toilets, we would choose smashed toilets every time. If only we could have that choice. Others prefer the historical explana-tion. For centuries all public buildings were symbols of an occupying power. But how long must the fight continue against the ghosts of the past? And then there is the social theory. Vandalism is the contempt shown by the poor for the handouts of the rich. But there is no evidence to show that destruction of public property is more common among the children of the lower than those of the middle classes. They simply work different areas. The poor vandalise public toilets, while the sons of the rich work out their frustrations on the fabric of their classy boarding-schools. The latest theory comes from the Left. The law places more value on property than on people. But surely the presumption is that people who have no respect for property have no respect for people either. Whatever the explanation for it is, one thing is certain. If man is built in the image of his Creator, he scarcely enhances that image by destroying any part of God's creation.

The energy crisis

Isn't it extraordinary how many things have changed in the last twenty or thirty years. Little things mostly that seem to have no great significance. That is until you begin to feel the loss of something fairly important in your life. And then you'll invariably find it began with something very small. I remember going to Mass on Sundays when I was a boy. And I remember the going and coming far better than the Mass itself. Because everybody used to walk then. It was a great time for meeting people. Now everybody drives to church. And we don't seem to meet so much anymore. There isn't time for much of a conversation between the church door and the car-door. The next thing you hear is people complaining about 'never seeming to meet anybody any more'. And they wonder why. You've only to look at the long line of cars, bumper to bumper, clogging up the streets after Mass in every town and village in the country to know.

The pattern is the same all during the week. Driving to work and driving to school and driving to the shop and driving to the pub at night and worse still driving home afterwards. We've become very dependant on the car, particularly in all the small towns where everything is within reasonable walking distance. Walking itself is fast becoming a dying art. The motor car has made going for walks a very uncomfortable pastime, if not a downright dangerous one.

Perhaps the Arabs have changed all that. It might well be the silverlining in that otherwise dark cloud – the energy crisis. Now that people are seeking alternative sources of energy, they would do well not to overlook that one source of energy we were all created with – foot power. Unlike all the others, it has no known side effects. For thousands of years, apart from the horse, there was no other way of getting around. People did a lot of travelling then too. There was a bishop of my own diocese who not only walked to Rome but drove his cow in front of him all the way. The modern package tour is a very far cry from the old walking-pilgrimages.

It was St Peter who gave what is probably the best and certainly the shortest description of Jesus Christ. 'He went about doing good,' he said. The amount of good he did took an awful lot of going about. And it was all on foot. We all know that Christ has a big heart. What we often forget is that he must also have had a great pair of feet. Without them a big heart would never get very far.

Spoiling the view

I was driving along the road, as they say 'minding my own business' when I spotted this truck drawn up at the side of the road. As far as I could make out it seemed to be loaded with garbage. I happened to glance in the rear mirror after I had passed. The contents of the truck were being tipped out on the grass margin. I had gone on a couple of miles further when it suddenly dawned on me, the man was unloading his garbage on the side of the road. He couldn't have been, I thought. Not in broad daylight on a main road! He wouldn't have had the nerve! I decided to check on it on my way home. Sure enough, right there on the roadside was this unsightly heap of junk. And it was still there a few months later. You could pick it out half a mile away.

Since then I've begun to notice how widespread the practice has become. I used to wonder one time in all innocence how so many car-wrecks came to be in such odd places like in the middle of bogs or fields. I used to think the big bulging plastic bags stuck into the bushes in some secluded places were the remains of some family picnic, carefully tidied up and tucked out of sight.

There are times in certain remote places when you get the feeling the early pioneers must have had, that feeling of discovery, of being the first to stand on this spot. But the illusion doesn't last long. A plastic bag, a tin can, a broken bottle brings you down to earth with a bang. It will never be said of this generation that we disappeared without a trace. I remember one of those lone sea-voyagers being asked in an interview what struck him most as he sat in his tiny boat becalmed in the middle of the ocean. 'The amount of litter floating round in the sea,' he replied, without hesitation. Even after a few trips to the moon, we have left a couple of tons of junk there already.

In the story of creation in the Bible, we are told that after each day's creation 'God saw that it was good', and when all was completed 'God saw everything that he had made and behold it was very good.' I wonder what he thinks of it now. 'And on the seventh day,' the story goes, 'he rested.' It is becoming the practice among a few at least, when taking the family into the country for the Sunday outing, to collect the week's garbage in a big plastic bag and put it in the boot for dumping in some quiet place along the route. If this is so and I have seen the evidence myself, it is surely an odd way of keeping the Sabbath holy.

Out of the mouths of babes

'You big fat bully,' she said. She couldn't be much more than two and I don't think she has more than twenty words in her entire vocabulary. And every time she throws a tantrum, she fairly lets fly with these four. Strange isn't it, that the first thing we all learn is how to express our anger. We spend our whole lives and even then most of us never really master the art of putting our love into words. I may be old-fashioned. Sometimes I think I must have had a very sheltered upbringing. Every time I hear some youngster use the four-letter word – and I seem to hear it all the time nowadays – I squirm.

There seems to have been a tremendous decline in standards in this matter in the last ten years or so. And nowhere more than among the youth. The four letter word must be easily the most overworked word in the English language. You hear it everywhere, in the class-room, on the playing field, in the dance-hall. I haven't been frontally assaulted with it yet but I'm often caught in the cross-fire. Not only are your ears assaulted with it but your eyes as well. There was a time when it was confined to the walls of public lavatories. Now it is all over the place. In schools it's carved on desks, scribbled on the walls. And if you don't wash your car regularly you may find it traced out on your rear window. It is not confined to any age group or sex for that matter. You hear it even in primary school playgrounds. It has almost the status of a new trend among young girls. Perhaps it is a logical development of the shirt and blue jeans and leather straps that girls wear now – the unisex style – on the principle, I suppose, that if they dress alike, why shouldn't they talk alike.

But it is too facile to lay the blame on youth. If their standards are poor, it must be because the standard among adults is poor. It is said that the Irish can cram more four-letter words into a sentence then any other race. Some people even manage to split a word with it. Young lads seems to think it makes men of them. And where might they have got that notion from? Permissiveness has a lot to answer for, here as elsewhere. Remember the outcry in America over the language Nixon used. It probably did more damage to him than anything else. I never could quite comprehend this moral indignation of Americans. It is a sort of double-think. After all why should they be so appalled at their President using language they tolerate among their own children.

'It's a harmless way for people to work off their aggression,' some people say. 'It's better than planting bombs anyday.' That is true. But who said we have to be aggressive. Language is the one thing that separates us from the rest of the animal world. It is God's greatest gift to us and we spit in his eye when we abuse it. There is a great consciousness today about pollution – of the atmosphere and the environment and rightly so. We might do well to include verbal pollution in our concern because as Christ said: 'It's not what goes into a man's mouth that defiles him, it is what comes out.'

As for our children, we are their teachers, and as the Rite of Baptism prayerfully expresses it, 'the best of teachers'. We should keep in mind the words Jesus addressed to the chief priests and the scribes:

Have you never read,
'Out of the mouth of babes and sucklings
thou hast brought perfect praise'? (Mt 21:16).

Going to the well

As every child knows, there are only two kinds of water, tap-water and spring-water. When somebody asks for a drink of water he means spring water. Going to the well for a bucket of water doesn't figure in the list of chores a city-boy has to do to earn his pocket-money. It is part of the price we pay for urbanisation.

In the sprawling conurbations of modern life the age-old distinction between spring-water and tap-water, living water and dead water, is becoming extinct. Technology has replaced it with hard water and soft water, chlorinated and fluoridated. Probably this is why environmentalists find it so difficult to make people aware of water-pollution. For city-dwellers the problem presents itself in terms of clean and dirty water. And what is dirty can be cleaned. So the ad-men tell us. If only this were in fact the problem. But as every country-man knows, it is a question of life and death. And what is dead cannot be so easily restored to life, even by modern technology.

Ecology is by definition about the surface of things. And environmental pollution is above all symptomatic of a more radical malaise. Man's thirst is not confined to water. Nor is pollution confined to his environment. The deadly proliferation of drugs in the modern world symbolizes the frenzy and frustration of our thirst for happiness. The original expression of it is the American dream – 'two cars in every garage, two chickens in every pot.' But dreams can turn into nightmares as Americans are learning from their drug-addicted teenagers, their fear-ridden cities, their smog-covered suburbia.

Like the alcoholic, we are caught in a vicious syndrome – the more we drink, the greater our thirst. The more the advertisers promise us, the greater our needs become. The oftener we sample their wares, the more we become hooked on them. The luxuries of the last generation become the necessities of this generation. The motor car, central heating, deep-freeze, private swimming pool. We never do catch up with the Joneses. And we never learn. Happiness remains as elusive as ever. Materialism is a polluted well. It condemns us to a life of drawing water and unquenchable thirst. What we need is living water, life-giving water. And that we will not find, unless, like the Samaritan woman, we meet Christ at the well.

Parables

That's my boy

No matter how often I read the parable of the Prodigal Son (Lk 15:1-32) I am always left with a vague feeling of dissatisfaction. Rather than coming away with the overpowering sense of the mercy of God as shown to the Prodigal, I'm in some way irked by his partiality, which is suggested by his exchange with the elder son. Fathers have favourite sons. 'This is my son, he can't do wrong.' I've seen them listening to complaints about the apple of their eyes and shaking their heads. 'You don't know him. He's not like that at all. He couldn't do a thing like that. It's just not in him.' And you, the teacher, the priest, the guard, the neighbour, are a nosey busy body, a crank. He might even feel sorry for you. And it is not so with all his sons. 'I don't know what to do with him, Father. He has my heart broke. I can't understand him. He's driving me crazy.' Could it be that the Prodigal was the favourite?

Or is it that we know too many elder sons too well? Lads who have stayed at home to care for ageing parents. And by the time they have buried their parents, they have buried with them the best years of their lives. Theirs was a hard life and if they had grudges it was hard to blame them. There's a coloured photo on the mantle-piece in many a country home, that shows him standing outside the door-way of the old home, surrounded by his brother and his family home on a trip from the States. It's a telling picture. There he is in his peaked cap and collarless shirt, lean, lined, weatherbeaten face, looking more like the father than the brother of the returned Yank.

Besides, most of us probably identify with the elder son. The monotony of our lives makes us resentful of the prodigal's swinging escapade. We grudge the sinner his good times. It's probably why we accept the doctrine of retribution so unquestioningly. What makes our lives a little more tolerable is the thought that our good times are all before us and part of them, which we can savour now, is that the playboys of this world will pay in full for their pleasures. So in this story the elder son is carrying the standard of all the solid citizens, squares, responsible members of the community, the salt of the earth, while behind the banner of the Prodigal huddle all that tattered mob of misfits, drop-outs, lame-ducks and the rest of the world's rejects.

The really puzzling thing about this parable is why did Christ bother with the epilogue on the elder son at all. Surely if the message of this parable is the boundless mercy of God towards the sinner, then by the time the festivities for the returned prodigal are in full swing, we've got the message. The remainder adds nothing except to divert some of our sympathy towards the injured elder son. Of one thing we can be sure, knowing the story-teller, it must have a point. He was a master of his craft. Look again at it, but this time if you can with the eyes of one of the world's rejects. A drop-out, a misfit or one of the many mentally, physically or socially handicapped. Perhaps this is his answer to their agonised cry: 'Why me?' 'Why was I singled out for a life of frustration?' 'Why should I have been a faulty creation?' The elder son's grudge is their answer. Like the prodigal it is their handicap which makes them special.

Four in the family

Hear then the parable of the sower. When anyone hears the word of the Kingdom and does not understand it, the evil one comes and snatches away what was sown in his heart; this is what was sown along the path.

Dick came to a bad end. His body was fished out of the Thames one morning a couple of years ago. Nobody knew for certain what had happened. There was talk about an 'underworld killing' and a 'gangland vendetta'. Those who knew him best back home in Ireland were not really surprised. He was always a cold fish. Even as a young lad there was a vicious streak in him. When he twisted your arm he made sure it hurt. His first protection-racket began in the primary school. The others paid him off with sweets, pencil-sharpeners and apples. He was afraid of nobody, not even teacher. Flogging held no terrors for him. He was hard – hard as a stone.

As for what was sown on rocky ground, this is he who hears the word and immediately receives it with joy; yet he has no root in himself, but endures for a while, and when tribulation or persecution arises on account of the word, immediately he falls away.

Thomas was different, very different. From the very beginning he was very religious. Religion had almost the same fascination for him that crime had for Dick. He began as an altarboy and by the time he was in his teens he was the curate's right-hand man in the half parish. Everybody said he had the makings of a fine priest. But he became a civil servant instead and a very rigid and conscientious one at that. And all the time, he remained a great man for the church, a daily Mass-goer and a regular attender at evening devotions. Then suddenly all that changed. It appears he didn't take too kindly to all the new changes. They say he hasn't darkened the church-door since the Mass went into English. Behind it all, he had no roots.

As for what was sown among thorns, this is he who hears the word but the cares of the world and the delight in riches choke the word, and it proves unfruitful.

Pat was the golden-boy of the family. He was confident, able and ambitious. At school he was a natural leader. At home he was a God-send. Very dependable in a crisis. If a relative had to be buried or if cattle had to be taken to the mart Pat could always be relied on to milk the cows and send the milk to the creamery. He was never much of a one for the dances or a night-out with the boys. Maybe it had something to do with being the eldest. It was no surprise to anybody that he did so well for himself. Everything he touched in the business world thrived. He had both the head and the stomach for it. Luckily for him, heart did not enter into it. Because he hadn't any. Whatever feelings he had for people have long since been choked to death by his greed for money.

As for what was sown on good soil, this is he who hears the word and understands it; he indeed bears fruit.

Michael was the odd man out in the family. People said there was no go in him at all. It was no surprise to anybody that he was the one who stayed at home. He was always very easy-going. Even the home place has deteriorated since he took over. But then he had more than his share of troubles. The wife suffers from nerves. Especially since the last child turned out to be retarded. And looking after his bed-ridden mother didn't help either. Still, he never complains. He would not think of himself as a very religious person, but his wife, his mother, his children and the neighbours are all reaping the harvest of his goodness.

He who has ears, let him hear.

Salt of the earth

He is the man we all lean upon without realising it. Every club has at least one – in fact, without him there would be no club. Yet you won't find his name among the list of officers. And you won't find him sitting at the top table among the nobs on the big occasion. He is never asked to make a speech or a presentation. He never gets his picture in the local paper. Never gets a mention in dispatches. When the laurels are handed out, he's not among them. The nearest he ever comes to recognition is the final tribute – 'to all those without whom this occasion would not have been possible.'

And in fact, he is the one on whose back we all climb to greatness. While we mount the platform and grace the occasion he does all the spade-work. Other men dream dreams, it is left to him to make them a reality. He gets all the rough work, the sort most of us couldn't be expected to do. While others jockey for position he gets on with it. He is always there, always available and always willing to roll up his sleeves and get at it – the old reliable. There is a sort of relish about the way he tackles the unpleasant and unrewarding tasks that always seem to fall into his lap. Most of the work he does are the jobs others took on but never got round to doing. He never seems to notice that others are shirking, that he's being made a mug of. He is not given to measuring what others do or don't do. 'What does it matter who does it, as long as it's done', is a favourite saying of his. Saddled as he is with a lot more than his share, he never complains. When the show is over and the crowds have gone he is the one you will find stacking away the chairs and cleaning up the mess, while the others still savour their glory to the last dregs.

The extraordinary thing is that he is not resentful. He doesn't be-grudge the glory-seekers their moments of triumph. He doesn't resent all those who cash in on his labours – the 'Johnny-come-latelies' who steal his share of the honours. When the compliments are being lavished all round he is not hurt by the extraordinary lack of appreci-ation for the long and arduous hours he has put in. Or if he is, he never shows it.

There are people like that in all walks of life. Nowhere is over-endowed with them. Most undertakings suffer from too many chiefs and not enough Indians. And it is the Indians we should cherish. We are where we are today largely because of their efforts.

We can all think of somebody in our lives without whom 'all this would not have been possible'. Our own very special Indians. That older brother or sister who stayed behind on whose back we climbed to where we've got to today. There are many, many more whose generous nature we have burgled on our way up. They are the 'salt of the earth' The sort of people saints are made of.

On the shelf

She is just the wrong side of thirty. and already they are saying: 'It's a pity about Margaret – a pity she never got married. And such a nice girl too.' Margaret knows what they are saying. And what they mean. And whichever way you take it, it is not very complimentary. If they are being catty, they mean she hasn't got what it takes to get a man or she is out for a good time – clothes, car and continental holidays. Or she set her sights too high and now she is regretting that she has missed the boat. Or she opted out of the marriage stakes because she hasn't got the guts for it. They are all wide of the mark. Sure, she has had her chances – more than most married women ever had. If she was selective it was because she could afford to be. It is easier to make up your mind when your options are limited. Her problem was the reverse. And it wasn't that she was too particular either. It was just that those who didn't pop the question were sometimes more desirable than those who did. And then the circumstances weren't always right either. She had to consider her widowed father. Somebody had to look after him. And then she was helping to pay her younger brother's way through college. Now her father is dead and her younger brother married. She didn't marry then, not because she was too selfish but because she wasn't selfish enough. She hasn't decided not to either even though her birthdays are beginning to frighten her a bit.

Now she hasn't either the energy or the opportunity to get around the way she used to. Of course, she is that much more careful. She has seen quite a few of her school friends' marriages and some of them did not work out all that well.

There are lots of Margarets down the country as well as in the flat-lands of city suburbia. We are very often less than fair to them. To begin with, they can do without our pity. You don't hear anybody say about the former British Prime Minister: 'It's a pity about Mr Heath – a pity he never got married. He'd have made a wonderful father.' Anyway, who wants pity? If they wish to get married, society should provide them with opportunities of meeting suitable partners or at the very least, not surround them with so many restricting conventions. It is astonishing how few places a single girl can go to unescorted – apart from the church. And she is hardly likely to meet her future husband there. Even cinemas are not safe for girls on their own. And if things are changing, we should not be so quick with our disapproval. When we allowed fifteen and sixteen-year-olds to swamp the dance-halls, we did not consider what we were doing to those in their late twenties and early thirties. They were deprived of the one social outlet which was theirs by right. Small wonder there are so many Margarets. Society, on the one hand denies them the opportunity to get married and adds insult to injury by disapproving of them for not getting married. Let us at least pay them the compliment of regarding them as people who pay their own way in society, like anybody else, not as some sort of reject or second-hand rose.

Remember Martha and Mary. They must have been in their thirties. Of all the people mentioned in the Gospel, these two girls and their brother were Christ's special friends. And they weren't married, nor were they likely to.

A different drummer

They call us aliens, we are told,
Because our wayward visions stray
From that dim banner they unfold,
The dreams of worn-out yesterday. (Æ)

He had a beard, when a beard was a very rare sight. He wore his hair long, long before it became fashionable, and there were many other much more important things about him that marked him out from his contemporaries. In fact, 'he did his own thing' long before they even coined that phrase. The more charitable among us thought of him as unconventional but the vast majority were not so tolerant. They regarded him as a crackpot, a freak, a fraud, a blot on their respectable little community. And they attributed to him all sorts of secret vices you would think their conventional little minds were totally unaware of.

A big city could have easily absorbed this sort of person. But ours was a small community. And like all small communities it lay great store by conformity. And they could be very nasty to those who did not conform. If only he had written a book, become famous, made money they would have gladly accepted him, even treasured him. We all worship at the same altar of success. In our eyes he would have then earned his right to be eccentric. But he didn't, and that is what really made him different. He wasn't fired by the same ambitions. There was a serenity, a contentment about him that bordered almost on other-worldliness. If there was anything missing in him it was the avarice and pettiness that goes into the making of the average, normal man. Mercifully too, he seemed impervious to our scorn. If he was hurt by our contempt he never stooped to retaliate.

This intolerance for the nonconformist is not confined to the small rural community. It is a deeply imbedded attitude in society in general. One has only to read the letter-columns in the newspapers to see how savagely we treat those who dare to step out of line. Ironically, the most bitter controversies always seem to be those concerning religion. So often there seems to be an unexpected viciousness about those who pride themselves on their orthodoxy. And why is it that the underlying assumption always seems to be that those who think differently from us are dishonest? Maybe they are out there on a limb because they are too honest.

Henry Thoreau wrote: 'If a man does not keep pace with his companions, perhaps it is because he hears a different drummer. Let him step to the music he hears, however measured or far away.'

168

Turned forty

John is in his mid-thirties and already he shows all the signs of dis-illusionment. There was a time, not so long ago, when he thought he could make things happen. Of course, he was never so naive as to believe that he could change the whole world, but he did think he could alter that tiny portion of it to which he had committed himself. And he threw himself into the struggle with all the enthusiasm and energy which only the young and idealistic can muster. For a while there was at least the illusion of success. Others were infected by his enthusiasm. He was popular with the young. The old were indulgent towards him. Problems seemed to disappear at his touch. It was too early yet to look for any real results. But of course, what he didn't realise was that this was the honeymoon period. There is such a time in everybody's life. People were reluctant to point out the snags, to remind him that they too passed that way. Perhaps the more optimistic hoped he might succeed where they failed. But most of his older colleagues smiled indulgently and thought 'He'll learn. One of these fine days he'll cop-on.' Which means that he will wake up to the inevitable futility of it all. Sure enough, that is what happened. As the obstacles began to loom larger, his enthusiasm began to wane. He didn't have the same energy any more. The late-night sessions, the overcrowded schedule, the too many commitments, and the too few results, all began to take their toll. Of course, time itself was against him. He was no longer the new man. The longer he was around, the more people became familiar with the less attractive side of his nature. They too could make themselves awkward when they wanted to, and sometimes they did. So John began to cut back, began to drop some projects, to shed some ambitions. The great withdrawal began. Now he finds himself on the edge of middle age turned in on himself. His main preoccupation now is his own comfort. His work is where he earns his salary, and he grudges every minute he has to give it. As for changing the world – he makes his own cynical com-ments now about those who wish to try. His own efforts in that direction have left him very sour.

But of course that is not how he sees himself. He has rationalised the whole thing. Don't we all? As he sees it, he has been victimised by the system. It is his favourite grudge, the system. What does John work at, you might be interested to know. In the class-room they call him teacher, in the surgery, doctor. Put a collar on him and he is a priest. In fact you will find him in any job that lends itself to great illusions. And where did he go wrong? He thought that energy and enthusiasm were enough to change the world. But it is not. The only worth while changes in the world were the work of men gifted with endurance. It was not the miracles Christ worked which altered the course of history. It was his crucifixion. and all he needed for that was endurance.

Looking after number one

He fooled a lot of people. And I should know because for a long time he had me fooled too. He was the sort of man that most people either envied or admired. He had all those qualities that make a man stand out in a fairly small community. He was 'concerned' and 'involved' in local affairs. He seemed to have a highly developed social conscience. And he did not spare himself at least as far as committees were concerned. He believed in spreading himself around fairly widely – and thinly. Before long he was a member of every committee in the parish from the Mentally Handicapped to the Town Development. Every night of the week he had a meeting to attend for some group or other. It was here he made his main and probably only contribution. He was a great man to second proposals, to back the popular causes, to anticipate the wishes of the meeting. His name figured prominently in all the minute-books. 'How does he manage to keep going' people used to wonder. Women used him to taunt their husbands – 'Why can't you be like your man?' The sort of person it would be easy to write an obituary about. You could fill a column simply by listing the associations he was a member of. Except he didn't die. He left us to join a bigger league. The last time I heard of him he was still going up. You should have seen the send-off he got before he left – a colour T.V. – no less!

It is only now that he has gone that the pieces finally fit together, that the real picture of the man emerges. He was a man with a mission alright – to get to the top. All his involvement in voluntary organisations had only one end in view – his own self-advancement. He was what is known in some places as a 'mé-féiner'. And at that point in his career all these committees had their uses. They helped him to make contacts, to get in with the right people, to make a good impression. He had the sort of job where these things can be easily converted into cash. All part of creating good-will for the company. It wasn't long before he caught the eye of his superiors. They took due note of this young fellow with the promising future. As they say around here 'It didn't do him any harm' – a typical understatement that suggests the locals were not really fooled by him either.

He is like a dog chasing his own tail – and some day he will catch up with it. And taste the bitter disappointment it always entails. Some day he will find himself cast aside like an old shoe by the company he served so well. And why not? He used them as callously as they

171

used him. And now they have no further need of him. He will become disillusioned, feeling, at the end of his days, like Cardinal Wolsey, when he said:

Had I but serv'd my God with half the zeal
I serv'd my king, he would not in my age
Have left me naked to mine enemies.

The hard man

Paddy Joe is somewhere in his late thirties or early forties. Hard to tell really. Because he must be about 17 stone. He has that clear pink boyish complexion that all pint-drinkers seem to be blessed with. Hardly a wrinkle on his face. Only the thinness on top gives any clue to his age. He has been drinking pints since he was about sixteen. He can down them now with an ease that is the envy of half the parish. He is what they call around here, with admiration, a hard man. He is married with a couple of kids. His other half is very much in the background. A timid little one – she doesn't appear much in public and never in public houses. Paddy Joe does not approve of women drinking in pubs. They are as different as chalk and cheese. She is small and slight and looks much older than her years. 'I don't know what Paddy Joe sees in her' is the usual comment you hear. It has never been suggested that there is any trouble between them. He is not afraid of hard work, makes fairly good money, and at least among his pub acquaintances, he is universally regarded as a decent man.

In recent years I've become aware of this cult of the hard man. The first awareness of it came from casual phrases dropped in conversation. 'He's a hard man, can down his pints with the best of them.' 'A bit of a lad.' 'No stopping him when he has got a few jars inside him.' It wasn't these remarks so much as the unashamed admiration behind them that staggered me. Surely a man must have achieved something more substantial than the mere ability to consume large quantities of beer and stout to earn this kind of admiration. Why should 'holding one's liquor' be a criterion of male prowess? And there is no question about it, it is.

I've seen young fellows, just out of their teens, arriving at functions and parties where drink was served, already fairly loaded. A girl is still expected to feel honoured if one of them lurches over to ask her for a dance. God help her if she refuses. It's quite acceptable to serve drink in your home to a visitor who arrives tipsy. You are failing in hospitality if you don't. Outside the drinking fraternity there is a sort of benign tolerance of over-indulgence. We avoid at all costs giving the impression of even being slightly shocked. The extraordinary thing is that in other matters we can be very easily shocked. Take sex for example. If someone tried pawing your daughter or making passes at your wife you would be justifiably outraged. We take a pretty dim view of somebody telling lewd stories in the presence of the wife and children. But if he is only drunk, we go to extraordinary lengths to show how broadminded we are. Even to the extent of plying him with more drink. Women are still inclined to feel grateful that it is the bottle, and not another woman, their husband has fallen in love with.

If there is a drink problem, and the statistics show there is, and a growing one, then the first thing we ought to tackle is our attitudes. We could begin by saving a little of that severity we traditionally reserve for social failings, for those who overindulge in drink. We could all show a little more disapproval and a little less broadmindedness and we might eventually debunk the cult of the hard man.

Identikit

His picture is everywhere. On television, on posters, in the glossies. He is the hero in every fast selling novel, the star of every fast-moving modern film. He plays the lead in every success story. And he plays a wide variety of roles. Top-executive, pop-idol, star-athlete, folk-hero, T.V. personality. He is the man everybody is talking about. Mr Success himself. The one we all yearn to be, model ourselves on and encourage our children to imitate. The new secular saint.

You may have noticed from time to time a drawing flashed on the screen in Police Patrol. It is the drawing of a man wanted by the police in connection with some crime. No photo of this man is available so the police have an artist draw a likeness of him based on the descriptions given by eye-witnesses. The result is called an Identikit picture. They can sometimes bear a remarkably close likeness to the wanted man. It occurred to me to try and do an Identikit of him – not his physical features but rather his personality make-up. What in fact makes him tick.

Above all, he must be bursting with self-confidence. Sure of himself and his ability. In a word, he must have pride. He must be eager to get on, anxious to better himself, striving to get to the top. He must be a winner. For him, only the biggest prize. To get there he has to be aggressive, rough-riding subordinates, trampling on underlings, ruthless with incompetents, unscrupulous with competitors. He must have drive. A man in a hurry. An angry man. He needs money, and he needs plenty of it. Money means power. Making money becomes his top priority, his sole interest. He must be avaricious. It may well be too that all his efforts, all his drive have a single motivation. Greed for the good-life and all that entails.

Not every top-executive or pop-star must have all these qualities to be a success. But frequently they possess four or more of them, to a marked degree. These 'virtues' which are high-lighted in every success story about the man on which we are encouraged to model ourselves are in fact what in days gone by used to be called the Seven Deadly Sins. Pride, covetousness, avarice, anger, lust, gluttony, and sloth. Or put it this way. No image-maker, no star creator of the present day would look twice at someone whose outstanding qualities were: humility, compassion, poverty, self-denial, chastity, abstinence and selfless dedication to the service of others, and yet these are in fact what make a Christian identikit.

There was an Old Man from Nantucket

There was an old man from Nantucket
Who kept all his cash in a bucket
But his daughter called Nan
Ran away with a man
And as for the bucket. Nan took it.

A sad tale that, but not all that uncommon. A financial expert would probably condemn the old man's handling of his finances for three reasons. Firstly, by using a bucket, he sacrificed any prospects of income which his money might have provided. Secondly, he neglected to spread his risk sufficiently and so left himself open to total loss. Thirdly, he took no steps to protect his risk. He should have insured the bucket. A neat analysis that but surely a very materialistic assessment of the old man's tragedy. His big loss was not the bucket, valuable as it undoubtedly was, but his daughter. And his great failure was not to insure his bucket but to insure his daughter. In fact it was his bucket's priority over his daughter that led to the final tragedy. Had he his priorities right he would have lost neither. If it was money that finally separated Nan from her father it was because it was money that first separated her father from Nan. And the day that happened was the day the real tragedy occurred.

We all have our buckets big and little. It's what gives us our ulcers and steals our night's sleep. It makes our homes tense and our work intolerable. It has a knack of coming between us and those we love; makes for us some very dubious friends and very certain enemies. It has a way of high-lighting differences, of widening breaches. The tears of mourning over departed loved ones are scarcely dried when the long knives are out over the will. And it has a genius for concealing itself behind a variety of labels. In Northern Ireland it is a Catholic versus Protestant; in U.S.A. Black versus White; in Vietnam, Democracy versus Communism; in Africa, Imperialism versus Nationalism; in industry Labour versus Capitalism. It may be overly simplistic to suggest that all conflicts are basically between the 'haves' and the 'have-nots' but there is a large element of it in every conflict. For the bucket we keep our money in, is a bucket full of prejudices, false priorities, impure motives, discarded graces. A real Pandora's Box!

It is almost easier, if one could make the intitial break, to do good without money than with it. It is not without significance that every saint began his journey back to God with poverty. But to be realistic we are not going to part with our buckets. Like sex, money cannot be done without. Tainted it undoubtedly is. The same money that hired a prostitute's body in a Dublin back street last night could feed a starving child in Pakistan to-morrow. It doesn't carry forward its sordid past. We should use it, tainted as it is, to make our daughters love us, our neighbours bless us and the poor and unfortunate pray for us.

Winking Willie

Winking Willie is not a bad chap really. In fact, quite a character. The life and soul of the local pub. Indeed, the pub is really his sort of scene. He's at his best with the small local audience. Has the gift of the gab alright, but that's not his real forte. He has the happy knack of knowing what his audience wants to hear and giving it to them. He drifts along with whatever currents happen to be running. He has no convictions, no principles, no affiliations. He's anchored to nothing, least of all to the truth. His aim is simply to please. And honour where honour is due – I've seen him in action – he's a real pro. I've heard the locals say he should be on the stage. But he'd be lost there. For one thing he couldn't mouth another man's script with any kind of conviction. And for another, the universal themes of the theatre are a closed book to him. He deals only in the superficial. A big fish in a small pond! Some cynics suggest a bright future in politics for him. But here again they miss the essence of his skill. He could never become affiliated to anything – especially anything as doctrinaire as a political party. He's a local character and that is as far as he'll ever go. In another age, he would have made an ideal court jester.

He spins a very good yarn. And like all good story-tellers, his are about people. The only difference is his are about real people and worse still, local people. He has a great way with words. He never says what he means and yet everybody knows exactly what he means to say. He has what they call a 'slippery tongue'! Everything is prefaced with 'I heard' or 'they say' or 'Rumour has it' and the more scandalous the tale, the more fervent his profession of disbelief in it. Ironically enough, his favourite phrases are: 'Isn't it awful the things people say' and ' You can't believe anyone nowadays.' He's a master of the art of innuendo and suggestion. The categorical statement he avoids like contagion. You could never pin anything on him in a court of law. He's a carrier rather than an originator of tales but they certainly gain in his retelling of them.

The extraordinary thing about him is that he's not malicious or at least intentionally malicious. And not overly uncharitable either. Truth, not charity, is his big problem. He simply can't tell the truth. Some people are alcoholics; others kleptomaniacs; others compulsive gamblers. Well, Willie is a compulsive liar. Somewhere along the line, he lost the knack of telling the truth. He lost his anchor and he's drifting ever since. I could well imagine, he'd be most annoyed if you called him a liar. He's simply trying to entertain, to please. And he genuinely wouldn't know what truth had to do with it.

Like the alcoholic, he has his big moments. He's in his element in a pub, surrounded by the lads, their laughter ringing in his ears. But he's a lost soul really. He has lost his credibility. As they say 'You couldn't believe the Gospel out of his mouth.' There's a want in him – something missing. What's called personal integrity. That's why he's so adaptable for other people's uses. A sort of village yo-yo. People hear what they want to hear and believe what they want to believe. And Willie gives them what they want. Like that of other handicapped people, his is a lonely life. All the more lonely because his handicap excites no pity. There's not one of those back-slappers he could call his friend. Friendships need trust and trust needs truth. And truth is what Willie is missing.

Why is he called Winking Willie? I suppose it's because he winks a lot. It's all part of his act. In the Bible, in the Book of Proverbs, there's a portrait of a scoundrel and it goes like this:

> A worthless person, a vicious man,
>   goes about with crooked speech.
> He winks with his eyes, shuffles his feet,
>   points with his finger.
> Always scheming evil, he sows dissension.

That's Willie, alright – winks and all.

Candle in the Window

A young Australian student is spending Christmas in a shabby board-ing-house in Paris. Like all students – but more now than ever before – his main problem is money. He has to keep to a very tight budget. His very slender allowance might have been enough five years ago but not now in the winter of '87. For him there is little joy in Christmas, sitting for hours in his drab little room or walking the streets of Paris to keep warm.

There is a young single mother living in a two-room flat in Dublin, under the constant threat of eviction. Without family, without friends, she lives only for her little child. She had to do without herself this Christmas to make sure that Santa Claus did not forget her little boy. And that was her only joy this Christmas.

And there's an old man living all alone in the West of Ireland. His family are scattered all over the globe. He lost his wife two years ago. He has nobody left now to keep him company at Christmas except a mantlepiece full of Christmas cards, and the memories of all those other Christmases when the house was full of children's voices and the smells of Christmas cooking.

For these three and for hundreds of others, Christmas is the loneliest time of the year. They will be glad when it is all over. When the fairy-lights, the Christmas trees and the decorations are taken down; when people return to their humdrum everyday existences. Above all, when they stop wishing them what they cannnot have because of their circumstances – a happy Christmas. For them, Christmas is like what it must have been for Mary and Joseph as they trudged the streets of Bethlehem looking for shelter and found there was 'no room'. No room then and no room now. And the tragedy of all this loneliness that surfaces only at Christmas-time, is that it need not be. Of all the ills that modern man is plagued with, loneliness is perhaps the worst if only because it is the most unnecessary. The one for which you and I are completely to blame. It is our selfishness, our neglect, our indifference which causes loneliness in others.

There is a custom in many parts of Ireland of lighting a candle and placing it in the window as a sign that Mary and Joseph and their Child are welcome there. There maybe a neighbour down the road who sees that candle and needs that welcome. As we lift our glasses to absent friends at Christmas, maybe we should look around our neighbourhood and see if there's anybody we have left out. If we can't have those we would most like to have, there is always somebody else we can have. Somebody else who is lonely because we don't think of him. Remember again the story of Bethlehem. The story which begins so pathetically with Mary and Joseph scarching in vain for a home to welcome them, and ending so incredibly with them entertaining their first guests, the shepherds and the Wise Men, in their first home, a stable.

The truth in her eyes

Maybe I was in love with her. But then, as far as I could see, so was everybody else. I cannot even remember now what she looked like. She was pretty – I think. I am not really sure. It certainly was not that that made her so attractive. There was something precious about her. And she had a way of making others feel precious themselves. She seemed to glow in a special way. She radiated a light that made those around her glow too. All very poetic! But there are some things, some people only poetry can describe and she was definitely one of them. I was only a timid, awkward teenager at the time and she was a young woman but in the words of Shakespeare 'Sometimes from her eyes, I did receive fair speechless messages'.

Hardened men seemed to melt in her presence and assume a gentleness that softened the jagged edges of their characters. In her company, one could see those tough, life-soiled men as only their mothers, wives or children were ever permitted to see them. She drew out of them an innocence even they themselves thought they had long since lost. Strangely enough, her effect on women was no less remarkable. Never a trace of resentment or jealousy as one might expect from them in the presence of a woman who attracted men around her like moths around a lamp. In fact, she seemed to make them blossom, more attractive. Whatever light she shed, it showed them to their best advantage.

Sounds like everybody's fairy godmother. Except, she wasn't that sort of do-gooder at all. Her sweetness was not the type that could be faked, her good nature could not be affected. She herself seemed totally unaware of her remarkable effect on other people. She must have been simply one of nature's flawless creatures which even by the law of averages, must turn up sometimes, however occasionally.

Her spell over me has long since been broken. Though the experience of it is indelible. I learned something from it which will never be forgotten. People become in some strange way, what we believe them to be. They grow in the warmth of our appreciation. Something we easily accept with regard to children. Tell a child often enough that it is stupid and it will become stulted. It will blossom forth only in a climate of love and appreciation. But there is a child in all of us that only the sunshine will lure out. Goodness is an irresistible force and when it takes a human form in the garb of a Francis of Assissi or a Damian of Molokai or a Teresa of Calcutta it transforms the world. Even those brushed by it ever so slightly, are changed forever.

Poor Old Joe

I'm coming, I'm coming,
And my head is bending low,
I hear the gentle voices calling
Poor old Joe.

The thing that strikes him most now is that people seem to walk so fast. At least, he has great difficulty keeping up with them. If only people would walk more slowly! Of course, it may be that they don't want to be stuck with him. If his sight was not so weak, he would have noticed on occasion, people slip furtively into a doorway to avoid him. Weak sight and poor hearing may be God's way of protecting the old from our insensitiveness.

That is Joe's predicament. He is old and retired, slightly deaf, weak-sighted and slow on his feet. He's not all that old – in his early seventies. Not all that deaf, nor all that slow. But just enough of all of them to feel himself a burden on people. Three or four years ago, he was doing a full days work and he was not aware then of any noticeable deterioration in himself. In fact, when he retired at seventy he felt he could have gone on working for another ten years. But he was glad to retire just the same. He needed a rest. A break from the daily routine would give him back years. A chance to do the things he always wanted to do. The leisure to take things easy and enjoy life for a change. His family was reared, his debts paid off. He had a little nest-egg tucked away and a pension to meet his daily needs. He looked forward to retirement.

And the first week, he did enjoy it. Ignoring the alarm-clock in the morning, lolling over his breakfast, perusing the newspaper, relaxed, savouring every moment of his new-found leisure. Then a stroll and a chat with the neighbours. Dinner, a nap, a read, a stroll, television, a pint and bed. Towards the end of the second week, he became a little bored. Then he began to notice things. That the place is very quiet and the time very long when everybody else is at work. That people always seem to be in a hurry, going somewhere or coming from somewhere. He tried to find things to do. Took up gardening. But he did not have the physical energy anymore. The crosswords. He did not have that kind of energy either. He had never been much of a man for hobbies – never had the time for them. Now, he had all the time in the world and nothing to do. There was a time when all he wanted from a newspaper was the sports page and a quick glance through current affairs. Now he began to read the obituaries. There was scarcely a week that he did not recognise somebody listed there. Death came to a lot of his contemporaries.

People said, 'He went very quickly in the end. Hadn't he aged a lot in the last few years.' They wondered was there some medical complication that had been kept secret from them. Heart failure was generally believed to have been the cause of death. What they did not know was that his heart failed because his will failed. And his will failed because he could not cope with retirement. Nothing in his life had prepared him for it. For more than fifty years, he had apprenticed himself to his job routine until it became part of him.

They gave him a gold watch on his retirement. The irony of it! He had plenty of time for everybody but nobody had time for him. He had to kill time. And in the end, time killed him. He did not mind being old. He was not afraid to die. What he could not accept was the loneliness, the emptiness, the rejection, the neglect, the unkindness. Above all, the complete unexpectedness of it all. They said: 'Death was a relief for him'. It was a relief for us too. We did not have to avoid him anymore.

The Donkey

There is a picture in my mind. It is of 'le grand Charles'. De Gaulle at the liberation of Paris, sweeping down the Champs Elysées, his huge frame resplendent in the uniform of commander of the Free French Forces, accepting, with nose in the air, the wild adulation of the crowds. Nothing very incongruous about this fantasy except that the General is mounted on a little ass. Nothing quite cuts a big man down to size as to mount him on a donkey. Yet Christ rode a donkey in triumph through Jerusalem. And nobody laughed.

The donkey has passed figuratively into the language as a symbol of the incongruous, the ugly, the stupid, and the menial. This ungainly creature seemed fit only to carry man's burdens without ever being worthy to carry man himself. Christ was partial to symbols. So indeed were the Jews. The point could hardly be lost on them. This animal fit only to carry their burdens, now carried their heavier load – guilt. The guilt of a people who had rejected their God. All their palm-waving could not disguise the shabbiness of their rejection. He was the burden they didn't want to carry.

Christianity has shown many faces in the last two thousand years. And by no means the least common of these has been that of the triumphal Church. Its obsession with power and the purple has done it great disservice. And we, the people, haven't been blameless. The measurement of our desire for its grandeur can be fairly gauged by our reluctance to part with these trappings of glory, even now, in an age that eyes it all with some embarrassment. It might help us, collectively and individually, to put things in perspective, to reflect on the fact that when Christ rode in triumph, he was mounted on a donkey.

Paddy the Irishman

A master of one-upmanship. With great ease and sharp wit he demolished his English and Scottish counterpart. He wins in the witty tales what he loses in the rat-race of daily life. Perhaps the creation of an inferiority-complex, of a conquered race. He has all the qualities attributed to the Irish Paddies themselves. A sharp wit, a quick tongue, a fertile imagination, a pride in physical strength and alcoholic capacity. A rough-living, hard-drinking, devil-fearing, gregarious bull of a man. On his back were built the roads and railroads of half the world. A friendly son of St Patrick!

There were other builders too who carried his name. The sons and daughters of institutions. The later generations of the Irish diaspora. More respectable, more respectful but still brash and boastful. They built cathedrals and parish churches, hospitals and schools. And they called their institutions and their children after him. There was a lot of nostalgia for the 'oul' sod' in them and a lot of 'look what we have achieved' in their monuments. And by their efforts St Patrick became middle-class, a gentleman, no less!

But all this trafficking of Patrick at home and abroad has exacted a price. And this is not surprising in a country where religion is nationalistic and nationalism a religion. Patrick has become a national symbol and the man who singlehanded converted the Irish has been well and truly buried beneath fifteen hundred years of national pride. 'It's a great day for the Irish,' we sing on St Patrick's Day. A national holiday.

Our ambassadors present heads of State with sprigs of shamrock. Our exiles paint the traffic lines on 5th Avenue green. And upon all this celebration we expect the saint to 'bestow a sweet smile'. It is the Irish we are honouring, not St Patrick.

Scholars argue interminably over the Patrician question. But the real Patrician question is concerned with separating the man from the myth, the saint from the symbol. Whoever it was converted the Irish virtually single-handed from the bottom rather than from the top, in the teeth of a highly-established Druidic religion, and all that without a single drop of martyr's blood being shed, which produced such an extraordinary harvest of saintly monasticism and which survived fifteen hundred years, centuries of which were of violent and systematic persecution – whoever it was, must have been a man of outstanding human qualities, and singular sanctity. A man worth remembering, a saint worth honouring.

186

Courageous he must undoutedly have been and energetic too. A man of great faith and strong feet. But in an age which prefers action to adoration and protest to prayer, it might be worth remembering that Patrick was above all a man of prayer. And that the last great non-violent revolution in this country was the work of a man who wrote of himself: 'the love of God and the fear of him increased more and more and my faith grew and my spirit was stirred up, so that in a single day I prayed as often as a hundred times and by night almost as frequently, even while I was in the woods or on the mountain.'

The End

Year-in, year-out

'Year-in, year-out, I work and I slave to give you a good home and a good education and is this what I get for it?' That is the kind of remark one hears ocasionally in the home when things are not going right, when parents feel in some way let down by their children. 'Year-in, year-out' sums up the long hours of drudgery and monotony which make up our lives, the unfulfilled dreams, the broken promises, the bitter disappointments. Above all, the inevitable and ruthless march of time 'that waits for no man'.

Year-in, year-out on New Year's Eve is a sort of official pause to mark the passage of time. We look back with a sort of nostalgia over last year and forward with hope to what next year may bring.

There is something special about New Year's night even over other nights. Bells ring solemnly heralding the new and ushering out the old year. A year when certain outstanding figures passed away. And, doubtless, when others too were born. It was a year of crippling inflation and depression. There were other happenings too which did not make the headlines but were nonetheless historic for all that. The year our youngest was born or baby took his first steps. The year our eldest got married or grandfather died. The year Paul got his first job or father retired. What the poet called 'the short and simple annals of the poor'. But then these are true for somebody every New Year's Eve. Now it is different, if only because we are traversing not only the last quarter of this century but of the millenium. Many of us hope to see the year 2000. Some of us doubtless will.

You can tell a lot about a man if you know what his attitude to time is. There are those who look back with regret at the lost years, who see only the missed chances, the lost opportunities. For them New Year's Eve means only 'another year older and deeper in debt'. The tell-tale signs in the mirror, the receding hairline, the extra wrinkles, the grey hairs. And the other more important signs which the mirror unfortunately can't show us, the closed mind, the dogmatic attitude, the intolerance of middle-age.

Then there are the others, for whom the day never seems to be long enough for all they want to do. The sort that never seem to grow old, who believe what we all think we believe but don't really – 'that you live until you die'. There is a man of almost eighty years, I know, who is learning to play the violin. Now there is a man who knows how to live!

Because there is no past really except in our memories. And the future only exists in our imagination. All we've really got is the present. No point in regretting or wishing 'If only we could begin all over again', because we can. 'Life begins at forty,' they say, which is only another way of saying that life begins whenever we want it to begin. Today, in fact, no matter what age you are, is the very first day of the rest of your life.

The happy ending

Most people are probably romantics. They love happy endings. Maybe they are conditioned by the fairy-tales of their childhood with their 'and-they-all-live-happily-ever-afterwards' ending. Unfortunately the happy ending has always been more common in fiction than in real life. In any case, retirement does not seem to fall into that category. For many people the latter years are a winter of discontent. The Bible so often speaks of 'length of days' as one of God's great blessings. In modern times longevity does not often appear a blessing. Many secretly hope that when their turn comes they will go quickly. Retirement for them is a very bleak prospect.

Such an attitude is not altogether surprising in a utilitarian world, where older people are expected to sacrifice themselves on the altar of progress. It is almost inevitable in a throw-away society that obsolescence would carry over from things to people. It explains the widespread reluctance of people to retire, when all that is expected of them them is that they vegetate to death, and that with the minimum of inconvenience to others. So acceptable is this view becoming that a Professor of Biochemistry at Oxford recently suggested that scientific research should no longer interest itself in those over seventy. Others are more tactful. They recommend retirement on humanitarian grounds. Let society place its heaviest load on its strongest shoulders. Let us relieve the old of their burdens. But in whatever guise it comes, retirement for many is not a very pleasant prospect.

And this is largely because most people have been conditioned to think of it as retiring *from* rather than retiring *to*. From their earliest years they have been job-oriented. School taught them how to become useful members of society. It fitted them out for a job. It placed great emphasis on ambition. It encouraged competitiveness. And the world goaded them on with its 'keep-your-nose-to-the-grindstone' axioms, its incentives for the go-ahead and its penalties for the backsliders. And in the meantime, all thought of that time in their lives when society would have squeezed them dry and thrown them out on the scrap-heap, was scrupulously avoided.

In an age of planned development, when retirement is an accepted fact of life in most occupations, isn't it strange how few people really plan their retirement? They simply drift into it. And isn't it time the schools woke up to this and educated people for retirement as well as

for earning a living? Even in a utilitarian society surely gradual retirement should be completely acceptable? Surely it is nonsense to pretend
that a man can put in a full day's work on the last day of his sixty-fourth
year and the following day be incapable of any work. And if there is
no objection to greater pay for longer service, why should shorter
hours for longer service be unacceptable? Such a change might go a
long way towards ridding us of our job-complexes. It might help us,
too, to put back in its place the real purpose of our lives, from which
there is no retirement.

We are, as Christians, pilgrims on a journey. And for us death is
the end of the road. This journey encompasses all the periods of our
lives. And if there is any high-point on this journey, surely it is towards
the end. Because it is the home-coming. For those who believe in the
Resurrection the period of their retirement combines the satisfaction
of a long road travelled with the expectation of a better life to come.
St Paul catches the mood, most congenial to a Christian in the evening
of life, when he wrote:

> As for me, my life is already being poured away as a libation and
> the time has come for me to be gone. I have fought the good fight
> to the end; I have run the race to the finish; I have kept the faith.
> All there is to come now is the crown of righteousness reserved
> for me which the Lord will give me on that day, and not only to
> me but to all those who have longed for his appearing (2 Tim
> 4:6-8).

The final solution

'And we who thought the old men odd, are now the odd old men' It happens to us all – we become old – and odd, too. The old do not become wise. They become careful. They have to. And careful people are cranky people. Notice how they talk about a man after his first heart-attack. He has to be careful. He has to watch himself. The old have to watch themselves and for that reason are not easy to live with.

What are we to do for the old people? I nearly said 'with' the old people. It is an important distinction. If I was teaching a language to foreigners, I would probably say: *do with* in the case of *things*, *do for* in the case of *people*. Regarding the old, there are three possible alternatives, four to be comprehensive. Three of these you do *with* the old and only one *for* the old. The first, I hesitate to mention, but it is suggested by some, is mercy-killing or euthanasia. Put them to sleep permanently. It is a horrible thought, but it has its advocates.

So is the second one. Abandon them. Yet, all over the world, we have the spectacle of old people, the fathers and mothers of grown-up families, living alone. There are excusing circumstances, emigration, lack of jobs or of suitable jobs at home. Old people themselves who will not hand over the place to a son, mothers who don't want their sons to marry etc. But whatever the reasons may be, the fact remains, they are abandoned. There is the danger now that what was forced on us in difficult times will be regarded as normal in these more affluent days. Leaving the old to live alone is accepted almost as naturally as young birds leaving the nest. Of course, they send home money and visit annually, if possible. Money can alleviate their distress but it is no cure for loneliness.

The third alternative is to institutionalise them. For a father and mother who have lived all their lives at home, in a family, their own family, it is a fate worse than death.

The only solution then is to keep them within the family. Perhaps it is old-fashioned but with all our progress we haven't come up with anything better so far and I doubt very much if we ever will. There are almost insuperable obstacles in many cases. Even the old themselves may resist. They don't want to be a burden. How well they read us! It will demand great sacrifice but sacrifice is the name of the game. Sacrifice is what a family runs on. And there are compensations. Old people and their sons and daughters sometimes find it hard to get along with each other. It is almost natural. Your father and mother,

when they are old, are very different to the father and mother you
looked up to as a child. And you, too, to them, are very different now
to what you were as a child. There has been a reversal of roles. You
are now taking care of those who once took care of you. There is
bound to be a certain amount of mutual disillusionment and disappointment. Both of you are living in the past. Your relationship is
coloured by the past. You are dealing with ghosts of better days. But
'it is better to be fighting than to be lonely', as Brendan Behan once
wrote. Grandparents and grandchildren have no such complications.
They accept each other as they are. And they have a lot in common.
Nobody should deny grandparents the company of their grandchildren
or for that matter, neither should the little ones be denied the unique
affection which the very old have for the very young.

My son, support your father in his old age,
    do not grieve him during his life.
Even if his mind should fail show him sympathy,
    do not despise him in your health and strength.
For kindness to a father shall not be forgotten
    but serve as a reparation for your sins.
In the days of your affliction, it will be remembered.
    Like frost in sunshine, your sins will melt away.
The son who deserts his father is no better than a blasphemer
    and whoever angers his mother is accursed of the Lord.

And that is the last word on the subject – the word of God.

Finding a home

There is no sadder sight than that of an old man hanging on desperately to a miserable patch of bog and stone. That it should come to this, that he should have to hang on to the home-place as his only insurance against abandonment, is a terrible indictment of the quality of life. There is enough sad evidence in homes and hospitals everywhere to show that those whose instincts tell them to hang on to whatever they've got are being very shrewd. Signing over the place for many was the greatest mistake they ever made. Indeed for some, it might well have been the signing of their own death warrants. The ink was hardly dry on the paper when the first moves to ease them out began.

And they began very often innocently enough. A bit of a 'flu one winter and the old man was moved – and very wisely too – into hospital. 'You'll be as right as rain in a couple of days,' they all told him when the ambulance came to take him away. The way he looked back at the old home indicated he had a premonition he would never see it again. And he was right. His bout of influenza left him very weak and a long spell of convalescence was recommended. 'You couldn't be better looked after,' his family impressed on him, when they came to see him on visitor's day. 'Sure, it's like a grade A hotel. You've only to press a button when you want anything.' It was a different story when the hospital tried to prevail on them to take him home with them. It was out of the question. They couldn't possibly take responsibility for him. What with the children and themselves, they simply hadn't any room for him. Besides, weren't they all paying huge taxes and weren't they more that entitled to free hospitalisation for him. The old man died sooner than was expected. His death certificate listed heart failure as the cause of death. But those who nursed him at the end knew it was heart-break not heart failure that killed him.

It is what a lot of the old in hospitals die from. They die from lack of love – the sort of love one can only get from one's family in one's own home. No praise could be too great to shower on nurses who care for these old patients as if they were their own. It is altogether unfair of us that we should expect them to give to strangers what we are not prepared to give our own. Life has a strange way of coming back on people. History has a nasty habit of repeating itself. Those who abandon their old people in hospitals, homes and institutions, may themselves some day be abandoned by those very children in whose interest they claim the old are now being sacrificed.

Of sound mind

'Whatever became of Michael? I haven't seen or heard of him since the day his father was buried. And that must be fifteen years ago at least. It's a wonder he never comes back visiting.' That's the kind of remark one hears occasionally in any small town about some long-absent friend whose name crops up in conversation. And the company exchange knowing looks. Eventually someone puts you wise. 'There was a bit of trouble over the will', you are told confidentially. 'The family aren't talking since.' You would be surprised at the number of families that have fallen out over wills and inheritances. There is something terribly tragic about a man who spends his whole life rearing and looking after a family and then undoes his whole life's work after his death by the will he makes or more often the will he does not make.

In fairness to those coming after you, everybody with property and dependents should make a will. It is the last opportunity we get of doing some little good after we are gone, and we should not keep putting it off until we are old and sick. Now is the time when we are young and healthy and death could not be further from our minds. God forbid, we could die in a road accident. Many people do every day of the year. It is an awful thing for a member of a family to have to go to a father on his death-bed to ask him to make a will. It is not fair to the living or the dying. It can seem a callous indifference to the plight of a dying father and an unseemly interest in his property. There are times and they are frequent enough when it has to be done. And God help those who have to do it.

There is a lot to be said for making your will now while your are still of sound mind. You are in a better position to get your priorities right. The old are prey to all sorts of fears and obsessions. Their loneliness can be easily exploited by the unscrupulous. Their minds can be easily poisoned against absent children. They can be and sometimes are unduly influenced. Their security might depend on who is going to benefit. Sometimes they are pressurised simply by their wish not to appear ungrateful to those who are looking after them.

One other thing, it should not need saying, but I'm afraid it does. Your wife is co-owner of all you possess. At least that was the undertaking you gave when you married her. 'With all my worldly goods I thee endow.' To die without making a will is to do her an injustice. To bequeath her a life interest in the property hardly seems a just fulfillment of your marriage undertaking.

THE END

When all is said and done about wills, there is an awful lot to be said for using your money now to do whatever good you can. Goodwill is better than any will. If you leave nothing after you but that, your children will have no reason to complain.

Should we tell them?

I remember well the night my father died. It was a night I won't easily forget for a number of reasons. About midnight, he got a coronary attack. The doctor was sent for and after a thorough examination he told me that my father was seriously ill, too weak in fact to be moved to hospital. The best thing was to let him try and get some sleep and for me to look in on him periodically during the night. I think I must have been in some sort of a daze. Only an hour previously we had had the usual cup of tea and bit of a chat before going to bed. The whole thing was so sudden.

Two things about that night remain etched on my memory. The first is that nothing, not even everything the doctor said could get it through to me that my father was dying, and secondly – and this I can now see as plain as daylight with hindsight of course – my father was absolutely sure he was dying and spoke constantly of it in a calm, cool, clinical sort of way. To explain my failure to realise the seriousness of the situation, let me add my father looked exactly the same to me after the attack as before it. If anything a little more alert and definitely a lot more talkative. Because everytime I peeked in on him that night, he was sitting up wide-awake and wanting to talk. And the talk always came round to the same subject – death – in one way or another. And I kept trying to steer him away from it. 'Don't be talking like that,' I used to say, 'you'll be right as rain in the morning.' But he insisted. At least until he had outlined to me what he wanted me to do with the little savings he had and who in the family he wanted me to take special care of.

I never really analysed my own attitude that night or indeed my father's, until quite recently I read some of Dr Kubler Ross who has made a special study of the dying. She makes many interesting points but to me the most interesting of all is that it is not those who are dying who are frightened to discuss that prospect, but the living, especially their family and friends. Even those who spend their lives in daily contact with them, like nurses and doctors, shy away from becoming involved in any discussion of death with a dying person. They all fuss about taking temperatures and tucking in the bed clothes, using meaningless though well-meaning phrases, almost as if talking to a sick child.

If it's true, as Dr Ross maintains, that at some stage the dying always come to realise it – and it was true at least in my father's case

– it would seem perfectly reasonable that they should want to talk about it. After all, it is the single greatest and most definitive event in our lives. It is not so much a question of should we tell them as should we let them tell us? Nobody in this world relishes the prospect of dying alone. Most of us who have courage enough to visualise our own death wish to be surrounded by our family and friends. Not by a conspiracy of pretence and artificial cheerfulness, no matter how well-meaning. It is the last time the dying can communicate with us. The least we can do is to listen to them and take them seriously. I'm not suggesting it's easy. But it is the very last favour we can do those in whose debt we will always remain.

Born again

Few events of world significance could have been less spectacular than the first Easter morning. The sight that greeted those two early morning joggers, Peter and John, was not the risen Lord, nor even his crucified remains as they had hoped to find, but an empty tomb. 'What have they done with him?' Mary Magdalen asked the first one she met. Mary who knew and grieved for the human Christ so deeply, could not see beyond grief and the grave, the risen Christ. An empty tomb. No more. The astonishing truth came later. Christ was the first born from the dead. He had broken the death-barrier.

The empty tomb explained everything. An empty womb after a new birth. Life is changed, not ended. Birth and death have much in common. The child in a mother's womb has a cosy existence. All its needs are provided for. All its wants are taken care of. Nothing can harm it. Nothing can hurt it. Its life support sytem is all but foolproof. But life is more than food and warmth and security. If the child is to grow to its full potential, it must leave the mother's womb. It must quit one world for another. It must die to be born. And birth like death is never easy. Most people enter the world crying. Few leave it without regret. The unknown holds terror for everyone.

And yet if the child in the womb could only have reflected on itself and its birth, there was nothing really to fear. It was well-equipped for another world. Had it not two little feet that could walk? Soon there would be great parental pride and excitement when it took its first faltering steps. And there would be other important steps to take on the road through life. It had hands, too, hands that would shake more that a baby's rattle, hands that would reach out to greater things. Eyes, now tightly shut, that soon would open up to mother's smile, sun-rise, a Renoir, flowers, light and darkness. Ears that could hear no more than the deafening drum-beat of a mother's heart would hear bird-song and Beethoven, laughter and love's sweet nothings and the word of God. Ephetha! A tongue that would speak, communicate and sing the marvels of creation. Its own little heart would take over life supporting and loving. But first it must die. It must be expelled from its mother's womb.

The world is a womb. Mother earth. The time comes when we have gone full term. Three score and ten is as normal for second delivery as nine months was for our first. It can be premature or overdue. Some babies cling to the womb longer. Some cling to life longer. Womb-bound they are reluctant to part. Parents, in turn, become dependant on life-support systems. Second childhood! Delivery is difficult for some, easy for others, inevitable for all. The cycle is irreversible. 'Unless a man be born again,' Christ told a puzzled Nicodemus, 'he cannot enter the kingdom of heaven.' There is nothing to fear, nothing to regret. When we shake off this mortal coil we will begin a new life, eternal life. We have vast untapped talents that can only blossom there.

> Eye hath not seen, nor ear heard
> nor hath it entered into the heart of men
> to conceive what God hath in store
> for those whom he loves.

Sorry for your trouble

'I'm sorry for your trouble,' you say awkwardly pressing the hand held out to you. Convention imposes these awkward moments on us and we steel ourselves to measure up. Mercifully, these encounters are brief. We may become almost as professional as undertakers at them. Besides, very often the grief itself of the deceased is little more than conventional. Their tears are already shed or perhaps still to come. And death itself doesn't weigh equally on all shoulders – not even when the relationship is close and the loss great. Occasionally, one intrudes upon an enormous grief and the conventional phrase perishes from the impact of it. It is a shattering thing to intrude upon another's intimate life, to see the raw emotion of a stranger. Only on such odd occasions, do we become aware of the inadequacy of conventions. And as every priest knows, 'the consolations of religion' are meaningless to the stricken. The great flood of emotion must subside before religion can console. Fortunately, the drama of death requires only solemnity from its masters of ceremony. And in circumstances such as these priests are only too happy to oblige. Only God and little children could share such grief. Christ wept.

Such must have been the grief of Martha and her sister Mary. And to think they might have been spared this heartbreak. Blunt Martha didn't put a tooth in it. 'If you had been here,' she complained, 'my brother would not have died.' Christ's needless and costly delay must have hurt. The bitterness of her grief was not to be assuaged by the 'consolations of religion'. 'I know he will rise again at the resurrection on the last day,' she retorted. Even the gentle Mary rebuked him. On that day in Bethany Christ met anger as well as grief.

Christ made no apologies. Did they not know that what they were asking of him was his life for Lazarus? Can even a friendship such as theirs demand so much? They must have known, as his disciples knew, that their cryptic message: 'He whom you love is ill,' was a warrant for his death. He who said: 'Greater love than this no man hath, than a man lays down his life for his friend,' delayed only to insure that the full price would be exacted. And part of that price was the angry tears of Mary and Martha.

THE END

That thy tears may cease

The strange thing about it is that people never regarded them as being really very close. Even in their more active days they rarely went anywhere together. Of course he was a good deal older than her. That might explain it. In any case, as far as appearances went they seemed more like a man and his housekeeper rather than a man and his wife. He was a gruff sort of a man and the older he got the more gruff he became. The neighbours found him very off-putting. Nobody ever really got very close to him. But he was one of them and when he died they all turned out for the funeral. Everybody was very kind. They called to the house and offered sympathy. The women made tea and sandwiches. The men helped with the funeral arrangements and contacted relatives. And all that time she remained very composed. Even at the grave-side her grief was scarcely noticeable. Some people even said it was probably a great relief to her. He must have been a very difficult man to live with.

But it wasn't like that at all. It was only in the following days and weeks and months in the privacy of her empty house that she really broke down and wept. In fact, it took a whole year before she began to pull herself together again. At first, she used to sit in a chair for hours on end unable to do anything. Every time she turned round she expected to see him sitting there reading the paper. Whenever a door slammed or a floor-board creaked she thought it was himself pottering around upstairs. There were even times when she thought she heard him cough or call. And each new realisation of her loss crushed her.

That this should surprise us is itself surprising. After all, she had shared forty years of her life with him. In fact, she could scarcely remember now that time in her life before she knew him. Even if their love was never of the hanky-panky sort it was none the less very real for all that. They had grown into each other. The man who was 'her other half' was not at all the man the neighbours saw.

We have a great reputation in Ireland for attending funerals. And justifiably so. No matter who you are, you can be certain of a decent send-off. They will all put in an appearance. Those who can't make it will send Mass-cards and messages of sympathy. And it is a good thing. It is a great comfort to the bereaved. We crowd out their sorrow at a time of great grief. But it is a great pity we don't stretch our concern for them over a longer period. Because it is only later that many of them really feel their loss. We could be a great help to them. We could shorten their agony and keep them from brooding, take them out of themselves. And all by giving them a bit of our time and a bit of our company. It is a great work of mercy. And God knows, it is not very easy. It can be very depressing. We all have our own problems that we want to escape from when we have a little time off. It is no wonder, among the great works of mercy mentioned in the Gospel, that the care of widows and orphans, who after all are the bereaved, is rated among the greatest.

Going, Going, Gone!

'May I draw your attention to lot 22. Here we have a very fine mahogany cocktail cabinet, opulent finish. . . Lot 25, one cedar stereophonic Hi-Fi record-player plus radio, 2 speakers plus a wide selection of L.P. records as new. . . Lot 43, one 18ft clinker-built row boat with 5 h.p. outboard engine both in good condition. . . Lot 65 one outsize black leather golf-bag with caddy-car and full set of Jack Nicklaus irons plus 4 Peter Thomson woods, all in first class condition.' And so the auctioneer drones on, efficiently but respectfully as the occasion demands, with the odd attempt at flippancy to relieve the tension. And so he disposes of all my possessions after I'm gone.

It seems strange now as one tries to picture one's own auction but there was a time when each and every item there was important to me. A lot of time was spent dreaming about them and working hard to realise those dreams. A lot of time was spent caring for them and petty accidents were fretted over and harsh words were said and tempers lost and others were hurt because of them. And we were changed because of them – more anxious, a wee bit more avaricious, a tiny bit more ruthless, a lot less considerate. It was natural to feel edgy when a friend began to tinker with your cine-camera or an admirer was fingering your cut glass. How we would bristle when the kids were getting rowdy in the vicinity of the cocktail cabinet? And we fairly froze up when a neighbour came to borrow the new lawn-mower. Those things once meant an awful lot to us.

But they didn't really alter us – or so we thought then. It was more a matter of respect for property. We appreciated good quality. We admired beautiful things. We had a good sense of value. Wanton destruction was deprecated. We took a lot of time and trouble to inculcate these virtues in our children – for we were certain then they were virtues – 'Daddy will kill you if you touch it'. Children have a way of exaggerating but they wouldn't be where they are today if they hadn't learned from us the value of things. I hope there will be no unpleasantness among them over my auction.

I don't mind admitting it now but there were times when I had an uncomfortable feeling, especially in the presence of the poor. The poor are a grace God gives us, a grace we often refuse. And the odd Gospel phrase that filtered through my tired mind on Sunday, disturbed me momentarily but was quickly swallowed up by the pressures of life. I didn't reflect too much on religion in those days, largely because I was afraid of the demands it might make. I realise now how right I was. Imagine how changed my life would have been had I taken this phrase literally: 'None of you can be my disciple unless he gives up all his possessions.

Rest in Peace

No warmth, no cheerfulness, no healthful ease,
  No comfortable feel in any member,
No shade, no shine, no butterflies, no bees,
  No fruit, No flowers, no leaves, no birds –
November

When I was a child, I was sent to the church on the 2 November, All Soul's Day, to make visits for the 'poor souls in Purgatory'. I didn't mind because all my pals were sent as well, and then the visits were fast and furious, with plenty of activity, the sort kids love. We dashed in, belted through six Our Father's and six Hail Mary's, dashed out again with one 'visit' complete, and one eternally grateful soul, as we thought then, rescued from Purgatory. It was a sort of game with us, the winner being whoever made the most 'visits' before the sacristan bustled us all out and locked the church for the night. We kept the score by keeping a dead leaf for every 'visit' completed. Underneath a street light we counted up our leaves to see who had won. And some kids were not above cheating. There is no shortage of fallen leaves in a churchyard in November.

I have never quite shaken off this association of the dead with fallen leaves. There is an anonymity about them both. Time sweeps them together in heaps in our minds. We label them the 'souls in Purgatory' and budget for them out of the surplus of our prayers. A prayer surplus now is even more elusive than a government spending surplus. To divide them into 'those recently departed' and 'the most abandoned', and split our Hail Mary's between them, is scarcely an improvement. The dead, like the living, are individuals. Individuals, some of whom were once persons of importance in our lives. Now they people our memories and haunt our day-dreams. They drop in unexpectedly into our thoughts. It would be a pity to let them go again without a prayer. They are part of us; they should also be a part of our prayers.

Our prayers for them, as for all the dead, is that they rest in peace and not that their memory should beget violence. There is hardly a newsreel on TV anywhere in the world that does not show the funeral of a freedom-fighter or political activist. Or a wreath being laid on the grave of some victim, innocent or otherwise, of violence. Perversely, we have fashioned emotive political demonstrations out of funerals. Using the dead for any cause is patently dishonest. Each man during his life fathers his own cause. Death is the end of each one's accountability. But as Shakespeare said: 'The evil that men do lives after them. The good is oft interred with their bones.' Some of them might well turn in their graves if they were to know what was being done in their names. Perhaps the time has come to lay one last wreath not of forget-me-nots but of *beget*-me-nots on the graves of the patriot dead.

There is no one whose roots are not dug deep in his local cemetery. It is a Christian practice to visit cemeteries and pray at the graves of families and friends. To neglect their grave is to erase their memories. To forget them is to forget a part of ourselves. Thurber once wrote:

All men should learn before they die,
Where they are going to, from where and why.

There is no better place to learn than in the local cemetery, from the graves of ancestors.

Epilogue

The Other Side

The other side? And in the last 2,000 years we have come no nearer to finding out what is on the other side – not that we haven't tried. Poets and peasants, theologians and artists, saints and sinners all have had their insights, their private revelations. There has been, at least, the illusion of progress. Every age (including our own) has been on the verge of a breakthrough. Each in its turn has found the insights of its predecessors hopelessly inadequate. This process of demythologizing old doctrines probably accounts for our optimism. Man has always had a passion for painting in the detail in the great unknown. His images of Heaven and Hell down the centuries have revealed more about conditions in this life than in the next. It is almost as if we hoped by stripping away the layers of paint, we might at last come upon the original. But there is no original and so we create our own. Precisely what we blamed our predecessors for doing.

A scientific age wants a scientific explanation of this mystery. Sound waves to replace winged angels! Ever since man first accustomed himself to standing on his hind-feet, he has had his nose stuck in one mystery after another. It was probably this great curiosity of his which got him up on his hind-feet in the first place. And it was certainly this peculiarly human characteristic which first brought him into contact with God and religion. When and if he ever loses this sense of mystery, he will surely lose his God as well. The 'death of God' in so many in our own time bears witness to this. He had to grope in the dark for ages before Christ, the Light of the World, appeared. If he had to grope since, it is not because of defects in Christ's revelation but because of its limits. The 'exterior darkness' is exterior and dark precisely because Christ placed it off limits. And not without good reason.

There is no evidence in this life to show that knowledge is a deterrent to evil. One has only to think of cancer and smoking or drunkenness and road accidents. And the anti-drug movement's lurid portrayal of the evils of drug-taking has had little impact on youthful drug-takers. Villagers continue to eat, work and make love while Mt Etna's volcanic warnings rumble in their ears. And San Francisco's imminent earthquake has not noticeably diminished their celebrated zest for life. The prophets of this world have seldom failed to issue ample and timely warnings of impending disasters. Their consistency has only been matched by the consistency with which they have been ignored. Prophesying, like weather forecasting, is a thankless occupation. If you are right you are held in someway responsible for the disaster you predicted. If the disaster is averted (largely because of your warning) you are dismissed as an alarmist.

But prophesying eternity is open country, and a fertile breeding ground for charlatans. The occult has an abiding attraction for man even in a scientific age. The message of the Gospel, to listen to the prophets is not an invitation to dabble in the occult but to accept the sufficiency of revelation. If you can't make it with that the private revelations of eccentrics won't help you.